# TRUTH CONNECTIONS

# Truth Connections

## An Understanding of A Course in Miracles

### Steven Dean

Steven Dean Publishing

Copyright © 2016 Steven Dean

The moral right of the author has been asserted.

All rights reserved.
No part of this publication may be reproduced, stored in a retrieval system, or transmitted, in any form or by any means, without the prior permission in writing of the publisher, nor be otherwise circulated in any form of binding or cover other than that in which it is published and without a similar condition including this condition being imposed on the subsequent purchaser.

Published by Steven Dean Publishing

ISBN: 978-0-9945916-0-9
Subjects: Course in Miracles.
Spiritual formation.
Spiritual life.
Spirituality.
Devotional calendars.

Dewey Number: 299.93
Cover: Michael Mchale

Typesetting services by BOOKOW.COM

# Foreword

In February 2010, I became a student at Sophia Holistic Counseling College in Western Australia and it was there that I was first introduced to A Course in Miracles by a fellow student.

After reading but a few sentences, I knew in my heart that I was holding the Truth of our earthly existence in my hands. After obtaining my own copy, I went on to study its vital message daily and devotedly from that moment onwards, never a day passing without my reading at least a paragraph or two.

In January 2015, I considered that I had learned enough to begin my teaching of A Course in Miracles and the idea of making videos and posting them online via Facebook and YouTube was suggested by my partner, Victoria. The first three videos being six to eight minutes long, I noticed that the shorter they were, the more people watched them. Wanting to reach as wide an audience as possible, I henceforth began making them an average of three minutes long and noticed an immediate increase in viewing figures. At the time of writing this, I had made eighty-two such videos and this book contains the essence of seventy-seven of them. I have ordered the video transcripts into daily (or whenever) readings and re-written them in a more conventional format as opposed to the original spoken word, renaming them as Truth Connections.

Steven Dean

Darlington, Western Australia. April 2016.

# Acknowledgments

Many thanks to Victoria Dill, Jane Rowley and Gerald Ball for helping me put this work together.

Special thanks to:

Jan 'Jango' Morrison for pointing the way.

Kare Fisher for introducing me to A Course in Miracles.

Louise L. Hay and Eckhart Tolle for thoughts inspired.

Dennis Waite and Gary R. Renard for the abundant inspiration gained from their excellent works,

'The Book of One - The Ancient Wisdom of Advaita'

(O Books IBSN 987 1 84694 347 8)

and

'The Disappearance of the Universe'

(Hay House ISBN 987 1 4019 0566 8)

respectively.

Jesus Christ

Without Whom none of this would have been possible.

All quotes from A Course in Miracles© are from the Combined Volume Third Edition, published in 2007, by the Foundation for Inner Peace, P.O. Box 598, Mill Valley, CA 94942-0598, www.acim.org and info@acim.org.

# Contents

| | |
|---|---|
| Summary of Contents. | 1 |
| Truth connection One: All About Truth. | 3 |
| Truth Connection Two: Oneness and the True Nature of Space and Time. | 7 |
| Truth Connection Three: On True Forgiveness and Nature of Existence. | 10 |
| Truth Connection Four: Coincidence and Synchronicity. | 15 |
| Truth Connection Five: How Sharing Happiness Brings About Truth. | 18 |
| Truth Connection Six: The Beauty of Being. | 20 |
| Truth Connection Seven: The Mind, Guilt and the Destruction of Evil. | 21 |
| Truth Connection Eight: The Abandoning of Fear - A Tale of a Ghost Train. | 24 |
| Truth Connection Nine: Oneness (Heaven) and separation (Hell). | 26 |
| Truth Connection Ten: The Last Judgment and Heaven and Earth's Passing. | 28 |
| Truth Connection Eleven: How to Recognize Your Unreality. | 30 |
| Truth Connection Twelve: Thinking, Seeing, Believing. | 31 |

Truth Connection Thirteen: The End of Memories. 33

Truth Connection Fourteen: Fear is in the Past. 35

Truth Connection Fifteen: Mankind, the Prodigal Son. 37

Truth Connection Sixteen: All are One and All are Worthy. 39

Truth Connection Seventeen: Awakening and Awakening En Masse. 40

Truth Connection Eighteen: Oneness, Giving and Receiving are the Same. 42

Truth Connection Nineteen: The Non-Existent Future. 44

Truth Connection Twenty: The Extra Spiritual Mile. 46

Truth Connection Twenty-One: Everybody is Everybody Else. 47

Truth Connection Twenty-Two: The Truth Has No Opposite - The Key to Understanding. 49

Truth Connection Twenty-Three: Visions and the Illusionary Devil. 51

Truth Connection Twenty-Four: Thank Heaven We're All Dreaming. 53

Truth Connection Twenty-Five: The Wholeness (Holiness) of Oneness. 55

Truth Connection Twenty-Six: We are Wholly (Holy) Spirit. 57

Truth Connection Twenty-Seven: Notes on Awakening. 59

Truth Connection Twenty-Eight: No Opposites = No Conflict. 61

Truth Connection Twenty-Nine: The Illusionary World of Laughter. 63

Truth Connection Thirty: The True Nature of Forgiveness. 65

Truth Connection Thirty-One: The Road to Awakening. 67

Truth Connection Thirty-Two: Think Yourself Awake. 68
Truth Connection Thirty-Three: Beginnings and Endings. 69
Truth Connection Thirty-Four: The Snake in the Shed. 71
Truth Connection Thirty-Five: On Origin of Existence. 72
Truth Connection Thirty-six: Animals - A Reflection of Ourselves. 74
Truth Connection Thirty-Seven: Science and the Illusion. 76
Truth Connection Thirty-Eight: No Past = Best Future. 78
Truth Connection Thirty-Nine: Prayer That Works and Finding the Source. 80
Truth Connection Forty: Living in the Past - Our Lives Were Over Long Ago. 82
Truth Connection Forty-One: Effective Self-Forgiveness. 85
Truth Connection Forty-Two: Spirit and Indestructible Water. 87
Truth Connection Forty-Three: The Illusion and Indestructible Gold - and a Spider. 89
Truth Connection Forty-Four: Thoughts on our Spiritual Evolution. 91
Truth Connection Forty-Five: Retaining Inner Peace - Deflecting Projected Anger. 93
Truth Connection Forty-Six: ACIM - Gaining Control of the Mind. 95
Truth Connection Forty-Seven: The Return of Oneness. 98
Truth Connection Forty-Eight: Spirit Guidance and the True Path. 100
Truth Connection Forty-Nine: A Brief Word on Reincarnation. 102
Truth Connection Fifty: Us, the Sons of God. 103

Truth Connection Fifty-One: Naming the Nameless (Within a Forest). 104

Truth Connection Fifty-Two: Glimpses of Truth - Tears of Sadness and Joy. 106

Truth Connection Fifty-Three: The Creation of the Illusion. 108

Truth Connection Fifty-Four: How the Illusion Appears to be 'Real'. 110

Truth Connection Fifty-Five: True Awakening - Seeing Through the Illusion. 111

Truth Connection Fifty-Six: ACIM Lesson 311. I Judge All Things as I Would Have Them be. 113

Truth Connection Fifty-Seven: ACIM Lesson 265 Explained. 116

Truth Connection Fifty-Eight: Thoughts on ACIM Lesson 247. 118

Truth Connection Fifty-Nine: What is Forgiveness? 120

Truth Connection Sixty: The End of the Dream. 124

Truth Connection Sixty-One: Love Loves to Love Love. 126

Truth Connection Sixty-Two: Black, White and Blue Men. 128

Truth Connection Sixty-Three: ACIM Lesson 326. (I am Forever an Effect of God) Ideas Cannot Leave Their Source. 130

Truth Connection Sixty-Four: At the Borderland - Awakening to Truth. 132

Truth Connection Sixty-Five: The Dreamer and the Dreamed. 134

Truth Connection Sixty-Six: Illusions, Truth and the Wholly (Holy) Spirit. 136

Truth Connection Sixty-Seven: There is No Death. 139

Truth Connection Sixty-Eight: All are One and All are Worthy. 141

Truth Connection Sixty-Nine: The Dreamer and the Dream Are One. 143

Truth Connection Seventy: A Tale of Labels and Tables. 145

Truth Connection Seventy-One: God does not forgive? Of course He does. ACIM Lesson 46 Explained. 148

Truth Connection Seventy-Two: Forgiving and Forgetting - Refreshing the Mind. 151

Truth Connection Seventy-Three: Understanding the True Nature of Cause and Effect. 153

Truth Connection Seventy-Four: Waking to Redemption. 156

Truth Connection Seventy-Five: Miracles 159

Truth Connection Seventy-Six: Bringing Truth to illusions. 163

Truth Connection Seventy-Seven: Above all Else I Want to See. 165

# Summary of Contents.

It is my understanding that when we 'die' the body goes back to nature as they are both part of the material illusion. We ourselves are of a spiritual nature and return home on our being re-absorbed back into the Oneness of the Source from which we originated.

Our brains are not actually 'us' at all. They are utilised by the spirit in much the same way that we use our computers. The computer isn't actually part of us, but it enables us to communicate. Our bodies, in turn, are not actually part of us, but are needed to navigate through the illusional notion of everything being separated into countless beings, objects and elements, that we are currently inhabiting - and mistakenly believing to be 'real'.

As we are born out of the illusion (not 'into' - think about it) with no guidance whatsoever beyond those who are already trapped within it, mistaking it for reality - and the one and only reality there is - is an easy thing to do. Not so easy to undo, but not by any means impossible. Our big problem is that back in the mists of long-passed time we have somehow forgotten what we truly are. However, at long last our reawakening to our True nature is now in motion and well under way.

Bodies are not needed in the spiritual Oneness of Reality. By Oneness, I mean simply that. Nothing is separated. All is whole, complete, eternal, infinite, unlimited and unchanging. The perfect opposites of a perfect separation - beginnings and endings, good and evil, birth and death, day and night, left and right, up and down, black and white etc etc, only exist here within this experience.

Oneness, being eternal, has no beginnings or endings or opposites of any kind. No opposites = no conflict. All is one and one is all. I know it is not an easy notion to grasp fully at first, but that's because the mainstream thinking of the world is so opposite to the Truth, as one would expect in a world like this. A world of chaos, as opposed to Reality's total peace.

Spiritual and unseen, peace, joy and happiness are enveloped within the Oneness of the Source. Perfect Love, its total Truth currently beyond our understanding, is the only Reality.

Having said that though, God, or the Source's, world of Oneness is detectable here even though it is unseen. That of His world cannot be given away, whereas earthly things can. For example; if I give a person my hat, I no longer have a hat. In fact, if I give away anything from the material world it is no longer in my possession. But if I give a person Love, Joy and Happiness, all extensions of the unseen Oneness, I not only still have them myself, they are multiplied many times over. This is because in the unseen world of Oneness, everything is one and giving is the same as receiving, just as having is the same as being. In the world of Reality, there is no lack at all.

Our way out is forgiveness in the form of recognizing that we are all inhabiting what amounts to no more than a chaotic nightmare and understanding that nobody has actually done anything or committed any crime whatsoever. The Truth really does set you free. A nightmare is only a nightmare until the dreamer awakens.

# Truth Connection One: All About Truth.

First of all I'd like to tell you all about what's happened to me since I began my daily and devoted study of A Course in Miracles back in 2010. The Lessons, 365 of them (one for each day of the year) actually took me 18 months to complete, with some Lessons resonating much more than others.

Am I enlightened? I'm not wholly sure, although many consider that I am, but I can definitely say that I feel that I am now living as I should be living. My contentment and happiness bears witness to that.

The Course showed me how to rid my mind of negative thoughts. It showed me how to demonstrate to myself that what I see around me is actually a product of my own mind.

In my subconscious, if I am feeling guilty, then I will project this guilt outside of me and it will create scenarios around me that will cause me to feel guilty again, like a Catch 22 situation. Whatever is inside your subconscious is reflected back at you. The Course has taught me that in order to have the perfect earthly life, you've got to have perfect thoughts—or at least as close to perfect as possible. Thinking as positively as a person can, goes a long way in aiding this process.

So what are perfect thoughts? Those of perfect love. To be fair, the recognition of perfect love isn't really achievable here, being the complete and diametrically opposing view of this existence. Perfect love is whole, as opposed to everything being separated as it is here, but we'll return to that in a later connection. It's all about being as positive as one can possibly be. But that doesn't mean to say that you have to walk around saying everything is great; "Oh, isn't everything wonderful?" and "Yes indeed. Life for me is exceptionally splendid." Especially if you don't feel that way. But what you can do, is endeavor to stop having negative thoughts.

Once a person stops harboring negative thoughts, they eventually can no longer project out of you; introducing a better view of life altogether.

It takes a while for this change-around though. But with practice, you'll surely banish your negative or guilty thoughts, or at least get them down to a minimum. It's very difficult to banish them altogether as the ego is very crafty. You'll go a month without such a thought and then the ego will suddenly dump a particularly nasty one on your head and you'll have to fight it off as vigorously as any ambush. Once you've mastered your mind though, you can project from it just what you want to project. Projecting only positivity is your goal. It's not only about only projecting positivity, it is also about not projecting negativity. The projection of only positivity will award you an endlessly positive life.

You may think, "Well, how am I going to do that?" Anything that makes you feel guilty is rooted in the past. All guilt is in the past. All worry is in the future. So endeavor to stop thinking about either of them. Just be in the 'now' where peace and contentment reign. You're only truly happy when you're in the now. If you are thinking about the past, as most people do all the time, it riddles you with guilt. You're not really living. You are just existing in a guilt-filled past. The past is of this world. You don't really need it.

It doesn't exist anywhere except inside your head, and even then it is just your version of what happened. Only the whole picture, taking into account all possible versions, can be wholly True. Most people feel guilty, such is the nature of this world, and even feel guilty for not feeling guilty. Well forget about that nonsense. You need to get those thoughts out of your head. The enlightened Eckhart Tolle, has spoken of his own tried and trusted method; basically, concentrating on and then expanding gaps between thoughts, but it didn't suit me. That was before I found A Course in Miracles, although I'd sought the truth via many other avenues beforehand.

You have to dismiss these negative thoughts. The best way to do it, I have found, is to stop a negative thought as soon as you realize you are having one. You can tell that you are because if you start to feel anxious or bad, or guilty or unhappy, then you are having a negative or guilty thought. Train yourself as best you can to dismiss it and then hold your mind empty for as long as you can until a more acceptable thought comes about, as it surely will. Stating "dismiss" and snapping your fingers can help to dispel unhappy thoughts. Try it. Practice it.

At first you will only be able to hold your mind empty for a very short space of time. Practice holding your mind open for longer and longer intervals between thoughts, not thinking about the past, and not worrying about the future. Keep practicing this until you are at peace all the time. No matter how long it takes, you will get there as long as you keep it up. You have literally everything to gain and nothing to lose.

I practiced casting out negative thoughts whenever necessary until I eventually learned to control them. Not thinking negatively is very difficult in a world like this. The illusional world, with all the apparent troubles it has, can make a person feel very negative indeed. Stop taking the media or any TV or radio news seriously. It is only one person's or a group of persons' view of a particular event, telling you what happened as they saw it. It isn't really what happened at all, as everybody sees things differently. It is all a matter of perception.

Another yet more effective way, but is really for the more advanced ACIM student, is to bring Truth to these thoughts - the Truth is that all thoughts are illusions and you are suffering needlessly. Imagine yourself and Jesus standing within the remembered guilty scenario and discuss with Him that all this is really no more than a dream. That methods works well once it is mastered.

Stop thinking negative or guilty thoughts. Not only does it give you a totally positive life, it aligns you with Reality. The unseen Reality, which is nothing but perfect love.

Perfect Oneness. That's all It is. Everything that's here is as One. Unlimited, changeless, endless and eternal. Here, everything has an opposite. Beginnings and endings, left and right, up and down, male and female, good and evil. It goes on and on. If you can get those negative thoughts out of your head, you are disconnecting from this world. Negativity is only of this existence. If you only give countenance to positivity, you then become of the Real world, where you and everybody really belong.

# Truth Connection Two: Oneness and the True Nature of Space and Time.

This connection concerns the avoidance of negative thinking, the actual nature of True Reality and what Oneness actually is.

Well, what is it?

It is the opposite to here. Here, everything is separated. Separated in a perfect separation into perfect opposites.

Black and white, good and evil, back to front, up and down, day and night. I mentioned it before. In this our world of separation, our biggest problem is the great big positive and negative that divides it.

For instance, in this world, it's ok for people to 'get out of the wrong side of the bed', so to speak. I grew up believing it was ok for somebody to come into work in a bad mood and subsequently get on everybody's nerves and bring down those around them. People would say, "It's ok, he just got out of the wrong side of bed this morning" and they were excused because being negative was accepted as being just part of life, the same as good luck - bad luck, etc, without them ever realizing they are actually bringing this stuff on themselves. As I said before, positive thinking will give you a positive life. I also said before that being positive in life will align you with the Reality of Oneness.

Now, what is Oneness? It is exactly what the word implies. It is nothing else - it just 'Is'. 'Things' are part of this experience. Oneness is no things - no-thing - nothing. Just pure spirit. Unchanging, eternal, endless Oneness. It is unlimited. It goes on forever. Not in the sense we see 'forever'. It just Is.

What is time and space? Time and space is an illusion we see that brings about this idea of separation. It is the exact opposite of Oneness where everything is just one whole. We are, in Oneness, of just one mind. Just as when I dream of people at night those people are all me, we are all God, or of the Source, within His mind, so to speak. Time and space is what creates the illusion.

Now, in order to demonstrate separation, the idea within the mind of the Oneness has to part everything to show that it is separated. In order to demonstrate that things have been parted, you must have space between them.

That's all space is. Literally just an openness between and around things to demonstrate that within the illusion things are parted and viewable as individual items.

This brings about a by-product.

Time.

As a demonstration, my palms are now pressed together to depict 'Oneness' and suddenly an idea comes within the mind of the Oneness. "Bang" I say, as my palms quickly part to symbolize separation and thus reveal the gap (space) between my palms. Time is required to travel between these spaces. If I walk over to a nearby log, it takes time. This time, or this having to go from A to B, causes my life. Being born out of the illusion (not 'into' it. Think about it), once we are within it, we have no solid idea of what it's all about as we grow into it. We are just given advice and knowledge, or at least what is perceived to be knowledge by the people who rear us, and also the people we experience throughout our lives providing us with what we call our memories; hence that which we call our lifetime. That is all caused by time. Memories are all about our movements through time. If there was no space, there would be no time.

In the Reality of Oneness, everything is whole, complete and eternally unlimited and therefore there are no gaps. With no gaps to cross, there can be no space due to nothing being separated. If there is no space, there can be no time, and vice-versa.

It is hard for us to visualize an experience where there is no time. Then again, while we are dreaming, we think what goes on in these dreams is true while they are happening. Temporarily forgetting our waking life whilst dreaming, we just 'are'. Despite what goes on inside our minds while we are dreaming - we, for instance, might be at a football match - of all the people looked at, seen, and observed, we don't question what their life histories might be or what their names are. We just assume they are what they appear to be. When, in fact, they were created in our own minds while we sleep. While we sleep, we believe them to be 'real', when they are actually just a dreamed illusion. We are in the same position ourselves within the mind of the Source. As we exercise our free will, just like the people in our dreams, and do what we like, just like the people in our dreams, the Source just Is, and awaits our Awakening.

# Truth Connection Three: On True Forgiveness and Nature of Existence.

More about the nature of this illusion, Oneness, time and space and what we are actually doing here.

This is a world of opposites. Everything here is split into two in direct opposition to whatever they be. I said this in the last two connections, but here I'll clarify. Everything here is split into an opposite; male and female, back and front, up and down, etc. The notion of separation being the dreamed cause of everything to have an opposite. Even colors have an opposite. Green is the opposite of orange and yellow is the opposite of purple, for example. Different shades of green, different shades of orange, they all have an exact opposite. Everything has an opposite. Except one thing.

Truth.

Truth here doesn't have an opposite. Nothing is the opposite of Truth. Someone could say, "What about lies? They are the opposite of Truth."

No, they are not. Lies aren't anything.

They are just talk of an empty nothingness. Like dreams, they are just nothing. And this world, this existence, is a lie. It is nothing, or unreality, in opposition to the Truth of Reality. Someone else could say "error", but what is error, but something not being as it should be?

Reality is Oneness. One whole, unlimited, forever eternal, changeless energy that we can't imagine while in our current state. It goes on and on forever, so it never stops. So it never has any gaps. So there is never any separation. There is nothing to cross. If there is nothing to cross, there is no space and therefore no time.

The opposite of Truth is nothing, which is exactly what this is. Truth is Oneness. Oneness cannot have an opposite. Otherwise it would not be Oneness, would it?

So therefore, where are we then If Oneness cannot have an opposite? The answer is, within an illusion. It does not exist. It is not real.

In the Bible, out of interest, it says that Adam (Hebrew for 'Man') fell asleep. It says nothing whatsoever about him waking up again. We are still within that dream, dreaming we are separated from the Source.

That's all it is. And when we go back to the Truth, we go back to Reality, as opposed to the unreality of this illusion.

There is one way out of this illusion while you're here, and that is forgiveness. Now we hear this all the time, "We got to forgive, we've got to forgive," and bloody well right we have! But trying to forgive all the negative actions that happen to a person all the time, how can it be done?

People can't do it. The very pressures of life living here in this experience are so heavy that very few can bring themselves to truly forgive using the nature of forgiveness as it is usually understood here. Most understand forgiveness to mean letting someone off with something terrible they've done.

"I forgive you - as long as you're sorry."

Which in a way, is sort of approving of the offence in some kind of give and take way and off they go and do something similar to somebody else. That little bit of forgiveness didn't really serve any purpose, did it? The only forgiveness that makes any difference and the only one that will get you home while you're still here, is forgiveness in the form of realizing that this is nothing but an illusion, a dream; and everybody in it has done nothing at all. Just like the people in your night time dreams. They might have burnt your house down, but when you wake up, they haven't done anything, have they? You might have thought it deadly urgent in the dream. You've got to get that fire engine round here right now. Yes! Quick! Dial the fire brigade... Then you wake up and the need for a fire engine is not there. You think, "What the hell?", then the dream is forgotten. Such is the nature of this dream we live in here.

The world is opening up. In the past few years, the last 10 years at least, I've noticed a vast difference in peoples' openness of mind. I used to talk about these thoughts a few years back and there was little real interest. Now a lot of people are listening to me. A very good sign.

Those monks who go and stay in those remote monasteries for 30 years, sitting there meditating - all trying to stop themselves thinking. Thought is of this world. The illusion is what your thoughts are projected outside of you, as I said in the first connection. If you're someone who feels subconsciously very guilty, you will project that guilt and bring about scenarios causing that guilt to be reflected back at you, seen as your everyday life. That's what this existence is. You make your own life up purely by what you project out of your subconscious. As I said previously, the key is to project only Love and kindness out of your subconscious and you're there. And once you are only seeing kindness and Love, it is because that is all you are projecting.

It doesn't matter what is in the news. It is not really in your life unless you introduce it into it. What's around you is you. You can work on getting rid of every negative thought in your mind and even every positive thought, to the point where you don't think at all. Just like those monks in Tibet, who have reached that such wonderful state of grace; where they are with the Source, yet still here. That is available to all of us by stopping thinking long enough for us to remember who we Truly are. We can't right now. We're so clogged up with thinking about all that is around us. While we're thinking about earth and everything that is on it, we're blocked off from letting the Source enter us. We talk of us 'finding God', or 'the Source', when really the Truth is, the Source is looking for us. And we are blocking Him off. He doesn't understand negativity. He understands Love. That's all He is. So positivity relates to Him; whereas negativity doesn't.

What keeps us here, is us believing that this dream is real.

The vast majority of people who ponder; "I wonder what the meaning of life is?" and to whom you reply "I'll tell you what it is. It's just a dream, or an illusion", will immediately pooh-pooh the idea and the door to Truth is once again slammed hard in their faces. Until they start considering that this may just be a dream, they aren't going to get home - not in this lifetime and quite possibly not the next one either, unless their new incarnation is of a more inquisitive nature, questioning their existence here. Their next earthly experience will come after they have been to an illusional afterlife which seems just as 'real' as this one and following which they will find themselves eventually coming back here again. That's what I've come to understand happens in these illusionary afterlives. Illusional afterlives are like this illusionary world. Anything can happen in them. It's when we finally realize that we are dreaming and that we are actually part of the One - We ARE the Source - that we can go Home.

This shell that we inhabit is merely cast off, and we walk away from it forever.

# Truth Connection Four: Coincidence and Synchronicity.

The very idea that this existence could be an illusion, to most people, is a totally alien idea. They are born into it and then brought up by people who also think it is real and we have no reason at all to believe it is not real while we are here.

But in fact, it is not real.

As it is an illusion, or dream, if you like, concerning separation into opposites. Quite simply, opposites will always conflict to varying degrees, and as long as there are opposites, there will always be conflict. This existence will never change. It will always be the same. It will get better though. If everybody becomes positive rather than negative, but that's another story.

What I want to discuss here, is proving to ourselves that this actually is an illusion. One of the clues we have around us that we often encounter is coincidence. Have you ever noticed that talk of coincidence is usually prefixed with 'just' a coincidence, or 'only' a coincidence? Which leads us to think they are not of any importance. That they are 'only' something or 'just' something. Or something that just happens just because it happens? In fact, coincidences don't just 'happen'. They are thoughts manifesting into form. What we see around us are our subconscious thoughts made into symbolic scenarios.

To describe it pretty accurately, the whole world actually is a stage. As Shakespeare once said, "All the world's a stage, and all the men and women merely players".

It could be said that we all share the same stage, same scenery and we all use the same props. However, we are all making up our own little screenplays in our own subconscious. Everybody sees the world differently. Everybody has different truths. What is true for one person isn't necessarily true for somebody else. There can only be one Truth and that truth is Oneness, which doesn't even appear to be here until you recognize it. Coincidences, or a better word, synchronicities, are the beginnings of that recognition.

Maybe you'll passively think about something unusual one morning and see it somewhere a week later, or think about it maybe in the afternoon and then see it the following evening. You might think about somebody, then see them the next day. Or you see something out of the ordinary and think, "Oh yes, I saw that on the television or heard about it on the radio. "

What you should do is look out for these synchronicities. They are actually proofs. When our thoughts go out, they don't usually reappear or manifest in the state they were sent out in. For instance, if an event has made somebody angry, this anger will radiate out of them and cause scenarios to happen around them to make them angry again.

It's like a mirror. It reflects back.

Coincidences, or the better word, synchronicities, as I said earlier, are the beginnings of understanding that this world is an illusion.

When next you come across a coincidence, think further about it. And start looking out for them. Then it becomes a game as you begin to realize they are your thoughts manifesting into form. You begin to realize that, yes, you are making up your life. It is just a dream and has never been anything else.

It would appear that the more passive and fleeting the thought, the more likely it is to manifest in the form it was thought in. Deeper pondering tends to manifest in much more unrecognizably symbolic forms.

# Truth Connection Five: How Sharing Happiness Brings About Truth.

Here is another way of recognizing Oneness, or True Reality, which is actually with us on this world as we sit. We tend to think that the only things that are 'real' are things that we can see or feel. Extensions of our Source, like love, joy and happiness are the True Reality. They are truly Real, whereas everything around us is but illusionary nothingness.

Here's how to tell the difference between Real and unreal things. Things from this world - the unreal world - if given away, you no longer have them. If I give somebody my hat, I no longer have a hat. In fact, if I give somebody anything from the material world it is then no longer in my possession. But If I give somebody love, happiness and joy, all extensions of the Reality of Oneness, not only have I still got them myself, but it is multiplied many times over and my happiness follows suit.

If I keep passing on this happiness in that the more people I make happy, the happier I become - there will be no limit to the happiness I achieve. And that happiness is from the Oneness. It is of God.

Love, Joy and Happiness are all of the Oneness. You can tell that because you can't give them away. You've always still got them.

The more you give them away, the more you've got. Whereas, in the physical world, the more you give away, the less you've got. That's because it is opposite. The unreal opposite of Reality.

# Truth Connection Six: The Beauty of Being.

A very beautiful place is a forest. It struck me that all those trees - some young, just saplings, some old, some long dead, they are all just like us, the human race.

Growing, reaching maturity and dying, falling over and rotting away. If the time scale of this forest was sped up you'd see a fine representation of the human race. As we are, actually... Growing and dying. Born, growing and dying, growing and dying, endlessly endlessly, growing, dying, born, growing, dying, and all for what?

For nothing really. Just for the sheer beauty of being.

Just being.

That's all it's about. And that's what we're about too - what we should be about. Just being, and enjoying every minute. Our lives are just as illusionary as we suppose the lives of these trees have been. From their births to their deaths, what life is it for them? Just standing there in a forest... However, all they require is there. It's just the same for us, really. Except we're able to move about.

# Truth Connection Seven: The Mind, Guilt and the Destruction of Evil.

The destruction of evil may sound like a great big task; but really, it's an individual thing. A person's evil is their own thoughts. What is evil to one isn't necessarily evil to another. It's purely subjective. Someone who blows someone up with a bomb is evil to the one who has been blown up, but I suppose the person who's doing the blowing up - for some reason, to even make him do it - he thinks he's doing a good thing.

That's the trouble with the illusion. It doesn't make sense.

When I say destruction of evil, I'm really talking about the destruction of hell in our own minds. In A Course of Miracles this is referred to as 'attack thoughts'. It's those sort of thoughts you have when you are walking along the High Street, thinking everything's tickety-boo, and suddenly an old memory comes whizzing in like an arrow from a bow - straight into the back of your head - ouch!

It is something that makes you feel very, very guilty, and it's come out of the blue; and that memory, although it may be many years old, will haunt you all day. That's your own personal hell. But nobody else knows about it, it is only you that feels guilty.

Nobody else can even truly guess the memorized scenario as it is for you.

So who are you feeling guilty before?

You're feeling guilty before yourself. Which is a nonsense - as is the illusion.

These thoughts are very powerful because of the nature of the illusion. Half of it is positive and the other half is negative. You can choose which side you want to be in. Those old thoughts from the past, they're the ones that cause all this guilt. It seems easy to say, "Well, simply don't think about them", but it is not as easy as that. It's not easy doing it, is it? It really isn't.

But it can be done. What stops people from doing it, is the fact that these thoughts are so powerful that people feel guilty for not thinking guilty thoughts. That's part of the great deception of the illusion.

It's not true.

You need not feel guilty. You only need to feel happy.

Guilt is evil. All evil is rooted in guilt. Feeling guilty about something you did. Feeling guilty about watching something you feel you shouldn't have watched. Thinking something you feel you shouldn't have thought.

They're stopping you feeling happy, those thoughts. Have you noticed that when you're feeling at your happiest, you tend to get one of these terrible thoughts creeping in that instantly destroys it. You feel too guilty about it to let it go, so you let it torment you. That is your personal hell and those thoughts are the real demons.

Demons aren't beings that walk around outside of you. Demons are within you. They run up and jump on your spiritual back without any notice. Even when you are as advanced as I am in ridding yourself of these thoughts, sometimes they still attack you when they think you are not looking. The ego is very crafty. You've got to learn to eject them.

You have to realize that it is these thoughts that stop you being happy, and these thoughts are completely unnecessary. It's only the thoughts themselves that make you think that that is so. Stop thinking them. You can stop thinking them by realizing they are making you unhappy. As you realize you are feeling unhappy, just shut your mind off as best you can and think of someone or something that you love, or at least anything of a more positive nature than what is trying to torment you. This way, the power of positivity is coming to your aid. The more you practice this, the easier it becomes.

This world is total happiness really. It is only its negative side that stops people from seeing it. For once you clear that negativity away, you see how beautiful it Truly is and that brings happiness. And the more it's cleared away, the happier you become.

I was told a story about life being something like a pond filled with algae and you only have a small rake to clean it with. But this rake is so small, that every day you can only get a little piece of algae out.

Every day, the pond, by nature of the algae, still looks the same. But one day, the rake will pull out the very last piece, and that pond will then be as clear as a bell, and everything will be very tranquil and clean.

That's how it is with working on clearing out your mind. Every day, rake away a little of that mess away that makes you feel so bad. Then one blessed morning you will realize it is not there anymore, and you are totally happy, and then you're living as you always should have been.

# Truth Connection Eight: The Abandoning of Fear - A Tale of a Ghost Train.

Here is a thought about the nature of our existence here within this illusion. When I was a young lad growing up in London, I always wanted to go on a ghost train.

I'd heard about ghost trains on the TV and saw them in films and it looked so exciting to take a ride on one. I had that child's longing to see a ghost and yet still be scared of such a thing at the same time.

Eventually, I finally got to go on a ghost train when a traveling fair arrived at Wanstead Flats, a common not too far from my then home in East Ham, East London.

There it was finally. A ghost train. At last, this great ghost train, with pictures of grinning skeletons and red–fanged vampires and all the other stuff associated with horrible and scary things was before me. I looked at it, and steeling myself for what was ahead, paid my money, got in the little train cart and went through the wailing double doors. By God I was scared stupid! There were things brushing on my hair, faces looming out of nowhere, loud screams and all sorts of aids to frighten and terrorize. When I came out the other end, I found myself uttering "Jesus" in an aghast fashion, but when I spotted some folk looking at people coming out of the end of the ride, I felt a bit silly acting all scared with people watching me. It was then I realized I was actually being afraid of nothing. There couldn't possibly be anything really scary inside this fairground trailer; because that's actually all it was - a trailer. Everything had to be fake. Nothing in there was real. After a hasty bit of re-thinking, I decided to have another go. In I go again and this time I was determined not to be scared in any way - and this time I wasn't. I came out with my arms folded in contempt at this ghost train and its effects. I now saw it completely differently and I hoped that the people who'd seen me come out saw me as someone pretty brave.

That little story is very similar to how I came to understand life now - that life is an illusion. Because when I believed it to be 'real', like most people do, I had fear, and fear comes from the negative side of this existence. If you don't have anything negative in your life, you can't have fear. That's why it is important to always be positive.

Fear keeps you here.

There's no fear in Reality. Reality is Oneness and only Perfect Love. Any time you feel afraid, remember: don't be. It's only a nightmare. Honestly.

# Truth Connection Nine: Oneness (Heaven) and separation (Hell).

In the Bible, on being asked what Heaven is like, Jesus said that it was like a mustard seed in that everything grew out of such a small beginning.

Well, a mustard seed is about about the size of a single 'hundred and thousand' sprinkle, so how would all of Heaven grow out of that? The Heaven that Jesus spoke of is Oneness and this is how Oneness works.

In this world, everything is separated into countless objects, elements and beings. It keeps separating and separating. That's why things get more and more complicated. No-one is ever happy with a really simple system for long. It gets more and more convoluted until it becomes entangled in its own complexity and starts to malfunction. Eventually all becomes unworkable until someone throws it all to one side and off it all starts again.

Oneness is whole, complete, unlimited, eternal and unchanging. Now I haven't got a mustard seed, but I've got a gum nut (6cm and round), and I've also got a stone, roughly the same size as the gum nut. Now all things here in this existence are allocated their own little space. This stone has its little space and no matter where it is, it's still got this small space it occupies. Nothing else can be in this space while the stone is in it. Same with this gum nut. Nothing else can be in that nut's space while it's in it. Their separation allocation.

But what if I could somehow force the stone into the same space the gum nut is occupying? Not so that it is double the size - like both of them together - the gum nut is actually in the same space as the stone. If I could do that, then what would the new object be? It would be half gum nut and half stone, but it would also be a new object. Instead of being two objects, it would be one object. Following that through, let's say I get a small piece of wood, and manage to force that in the same space as the new object. This new object is now made of stone, wood and gum nut and they become yet another new object. What once were three, now are one. Now, let's go on and on and on until we have forced everything in the universe into the little space that was once just the gum nut's space.

In a way, this gum nut is that seed Jesus spoke of. If you could put everything into one little space, it would be Oneness, it would become One. It becomes True.

When the True became false (i.e. this dream of separation we currently inhabit began), everything sprang from it - possibly in a 'big bang' - to what we see around us. It is all just an illusion. When we finally wake up, we'll see it for exactly what it is.

The illusion that it is.

# Truth Connection Ten: The Last Judgment and Heaven and Earth's Passing.

For this connection, I would like to talk about a couple of statements that Jesus made that are recorded in the Bible.

The first thing is when he talked about the Last Judgment. The church, or any religion, makes out the Last Judgment to be one of God; they say God makes the judgment. His Last Judgment is considered to be along the lines of whether we've been 'good' or 'bad', or whether we'll go to heaven or hell; something like that, which is not the case. Heaven and hell are two opposites, so they belong to this world, *not* Reality - the Reality of Oneness. There's no judgment in Oneness, because there is only One thing, so to speak. To judge anything, you've got to judge one thing against another; or judge whether they were right or they were wrong, but they are two opposites and do not exist in Reality. Therefore judgment doesn't even exist in Heaven, or Oneness. What Jesus meant, is the Last Judgment, or day of the Last Judgment, is when we (or the last person alive, being the last person left dreaming) finally judge that this is an illusion and we go Home. We judge between the Truth, or a lie. This is the lie and we judge the Truth. We make our Last Judgment and then we go Home.

That is all that means. The Last Judgment is ours.

The other statement is, "Heaven and earth will pass away, but my words will never pass away." This means that Heaven and earth will cease to exist as separate states. Here, we have illusion and Reality and they are two separate states. Even though the illusion is an illusion, it is still seen as a state. When Heaven and earth eventually pass away, the illusion and Reality, being merely a term used to differentiate between the two, will pass away as such and become One again. Jesus said, 'My Truth will never pass away,' because once they are seen as the true state of Oneness that they are, the Truth is revealed. His words are the Truth. It really is as simple as that.

# Truth Connection Eleven: How to Recognize Your Unreality.

Reflecting on reality and unreality, as we understand it, that which surrounds us is 'real', by earthly understanding. In fact, it is not. This is the unreal. It is the opposite. Oneness is Real. *So how is this not real then?* you may ask. But simply, when is it ever real?

When you started reading this paragraph, where has that instant gone? It has passed into our memories. And are they real? No, they are just images in your head. They are not real.

And the moment just passed where I asked that last question. Where has that gone? Into your head. It's not real. Put your hand up in front of your face. As you see it, it appears to be real, but when you put your hand down again, that image is now in your memory and it is not real. So when is it ever real? The answer is: it is never real, because this is the world of the unreal; an illusion.

# Truth Connection Twelve: Thinking, Seeing, Believing.

I was walking through the bush one day, observing the cows in a nearby field, when it occurred to me that, along with the trees, and the bush itself and all the shrubs, parrot bushes and the wattles, the kangaroos, numbats, lizards and snakes, not one of them had a clue what I was doing.

Not one of those creatures and plants, nor the road I was walking on, the dogs I was walking with, or any life form around me, had a clue about what I was doing, or what I was about. The world is totally and utterly neutral. It's a total empty stage with all the scenery and props supplied. I said this before in an earlier connection, but it's just struck me what a strong point this is. Everything is totally neutral. Absolutely. Any story attached to it is the one I am attaching to it. Even the people I meet, their doings in my life or their connections to me, are purely what I accord them. Thoughts about what their concerns with me are, and what I think they themselves are about, are of my own making. My whole life is a figment of my imagination. All the information is stored from birth up to this present point, and it is what I call my life. When I speak to my siblings about my life, they remember incidents I can't remember at all, and vice-versa.

Does that mean those incidents didn't happen in my life? Of course they happened, but I can't remember anything about them. If I was to write my memoirs, they wouldn't be in it, unless I'd asked my sister or my brother about such things. This means there are plenty of other things throughout my life I can't remember. Therefore, my memories of what life was about, are very much a patchwork quilt. It's not real. It isn't what really happened. If somebody had been in a position to witness my entire life, they would have seen it a tad different to how I see it. It isn't real, except from my perspective or perception. Even then it is only 'real' in the sense that it exists within the illusion.

What I perceive it to be, is what it is for me. And that goes for everybody - what you perceive it to be, it is for you. In fact, it is nothing; just an empty, meaningless, neutral stage, waiting for us to apply some meaning to it. Once again, it's just an illusion.

# Truth Connection Thirteen: The End of Memories.

**N**ARRATION from a City Churchyard.

Today I find myself in a City Cemetery where I've come to visit a certain grave. While I've been here, I've been looking around at all the gravestones. All these passed-on people, all these past lives, all of them now forgotten. Well, not forgotten completely. Like it says on one gravestone, "There is a golden chain that binds us 'til we meet again". That's wonderful. "Loving, cherished memories", says another. If you consider all these stones as a monument to a person's life, that life is all condensed into that stone, so to speak, and no-one really knows what his life wholly contained except him. Only you know what really went on in your life.

I had a bachelor uncle who died some years ago and me and my brother went to clean out his room in the house where he had lived with his old mum for seventy-odd years. In his drawers and dressers, amongst his belongings, were trinkets, key-rings, photographs, pens and assorted bits and pieces; mementos that meant a lot to him, but meant absolutely nothing to anybody else.

We were welcome to take whatever we wanted. I took a hat, my brother took a carpentry plane and all the rest went into a skip to be disposed of, because most of it was junk that didn't mean anything to anybody except him. He was the key to it all.

Every single one of the gravestones in the cemetery is the key to a life now passed and only those names will ever know what it was all about. A separate life in a separated world. Some will proceed to an illusionary afterlife, because if you believe this illusion to be 'real', you will tend to go to an illusionary afterlife to match, so I believe. I understand it works out that way as far as I can see, but I am only really concerned with the reality of Oneness, rather than what goes on in the illusion.

If you still believe this earthly life to be 'real', the chances are you'll come back here again, because you will mistakenly believe the illusionary afterlife to be a real heaven, just as most believe this life to 'real'. However, if everybody and everything is still separated in it, it can't be. It's not until we're all back to one again, to One being, to the wholly changeless, unlimited entity that Oneness is, that we're truly Home. Until that time, this graveyard will always be here, as monuments to memories that are now no more.

# Truth Connection Fourteen: Fear is in the Past.

In this connection, I would like to say a few words about fear. The whole world lives in fear. You know where this fear comes from?

From the memory.

When people look back into their memories - every day, every second - they undoubtedly always come across fear and this fear always messes up their world. Fear is rooted in guilt. You look back at these old memories and you feel guilty. The subconscious doesn't understand the past or the future; they are just ideas. When it presents old memories back to you, it presents them as if they are happening now, and we react to them as if they are happening now. That's why you feel guilty. You didn't feel guilty when the act that is bothering you was carried out, because at the time, it was the right thing to do as far as you were concerned, but now you feel guilty and you can't do anything about it. That guilt just hangs there.

It is vital that you get rid of this guilt because it causes you to subconsciously fear punishment and you don't know what form this punishment is going to take, or from which direction it is going to arrive. So everybody walks around in this kind of unwitting fear, all caused by their personal past, or any past. The only way out is to forget the past. Then it isn't there. Just like there's no future. There is only the now. Right this instant is all there is.

# Truth Connection Fifteen: Mankind, the Prodigal Son.

In this connection, I'd like to discuss Oneness, the Source, us and the ego. First of all, the Source is Oneness. The Oneness I speak of is God, but I prefer to refer to God as the Source, because the word 'God' tends to conjure up a giant white-haired bloke with a long beard and sandals, walking around on clouds and stuff. No, it is nothing like that. He/She/It is only Perfect Love. Nameless in Oneness as there is nothing else in Reality to address Him/Her/It.

There are some things that identify with Him however, the Holy Trinity, for instance. The first is God and the second is us who are God's son. The lost son; the people in the dream. We the sons of God in the same way that people in our dreams at night are the sons of us. It could be described that way and that's how we are being described - as being the sons of the Source, or 'God', as we are just figures in His/our dream.

Then thirdly we have the Holy Conduit, or Jesus, or Buddha, or Mohammed, and other such Spiritually higher beings. They were all conduits, because they knew the Truth. A conduit is something that passes on a message, a flow. He passes on a message as a messenger. Jesus passes on the Truth, which comes from Oneness, which is the whole Truth, so He's the third party, but really they are the One thing. Oneness cannot have an opposite, as then it wouldn't be 'oneness', so any seemingly opposing existence can only be an illusion - and anything that happens in that illusion is unreal. However, the problem still has to be solved. So the Real - Jesus, if you like - had to enter the unreal to solve it.

Jesus's story of the Prodigal Son explains it quite clearly. Think of the father as Oneness, the prodigal son as us, the fragmented Son of God (when I say fragmented, I mean, as we are, split into billions of individuals who all believe they are individuals when in fact they are just one within a mind), and the ego, which is the brother.

Of course, we, the human race, have squandered everything as we do every day, and we've got nothing left. We think we're going to be punished by God because we have been so 'evil', when in fact we have been nothing of the sort - we have merely been in a dream. The brother, or ego, who has worked for his father all his life, is very resentful and envious, because that's what the negative side of us is like. It is negative and envious and wants punishment or even death. That is the negative side of us - the hell side of this existence. But of course, the ego wants his brother punished.

However, instead, Oneness, God, wants to celebrate. Of course He does, His son has come home. He's woken up. He's realized it was a dream and the Source has to worry no more. As for the ego, it can complain, but really it doesn't even exist, and it knows it. Let's face it, that's why it complains - it isn't real. That's what Jesus meant with the tale of the prodigal son. Think of it that way, as I've just explained it, and it all makes perfect sense. Dream on.

# Truth Connection Sixteen: All are One and All are Worthy.

This connection is about people feeling unworthy and how to counteract these totally unnecessary and painful thoughts.

Unworthiness is due to feeling self-guilt. When you forgive, you have to forget your own past, but you also have to forgive everybody else's past too. You have to forget the past entirely. It's remembering about your own past that makes you feel unworthy. I'm not saying you are unworthy, it's just that in everybody's past, there are things they regret. I'd be very surprised if there's a person living that hasn't got something in their past that they don't feel guilty about. If that is indeed so, if they've ever felt guilty, then at some stage, they have felt unworthy. Unfortunately, guilt plays a great big part in this existence of ours. Thus, so does unworthiness.

The answer again, is to forgive your own past just as you forgive everybody else's past. You forgive everything here. Simply everything. And you forgive it by realizing that it isn't 'real', that it never was real, and that it never will be real.

It is only 'real' now, because you are dreaming it is 'real'. It is not forever. Only Oneness is forever. And we've got that to look forward to.

# Truth Connection Seventeen: Awakening and Awakening En Masse.

I'D like to speak a little bit further about the nature of the dream - or illusion - or celestial idea, however it may be referred to. Each one of us is having the same dream as I've mentioned before in previous connections, but each one of us is the same person. In the same way that the people we dream of at night are all us, each one of us is within the Source, as part of Him.

Each one of us is God, or the Source. Each one of us is dreaming about everybody else. That's why I say when we're sharing the same stage, using the same props and the same scenery, we're all making up our own screenplays.

An interesting thing about it though, is that while I am asleep, so to speak, or, believing this is real, everybody in my dream believes it is real as well. They are in my dream thinking it's real because I am thinking it is real. When I awaken totally, the people in my dream must wake up, and that's everybody around me. And that goes for everybody else too. Whoever wakes up, those around them must wake with them.

They must do.

## Truth Connections

When I wake in the morning, the people in my dreams at night disappear. They are absorbed back into me. For them, it is no more. But it doesn't matter, it was only a dream anyway. It doesn't matter at all. There are very few who awaken immediately, and realize the Truth. In Truth, awakening is a very slow process.

Because the Truth is so different to what you think is true, it takes a long time for your brain to get used to the information and to understand it. That's why, as I gradually awaken, the people in communication with me, and those who understand me, are gradually awakening as well. Truly the world is waking up. These are great times. Enjoy your dream though, for that's all it is.

# Truth Connection Eighteen: Oneness, Giving and Receiving are the Same.

I would like to say a few things about Oneness, because Oneness means exactly what it implies and within it, giving is the same as receiving. Just as having is the same as being. That's how giving love to people multiplies. Unseen extensions of the Source, like love, joy and happiness, once they are given - once you see that they are handed over and are seen apparent in the faces or in the joy of the people you give this happiness to, your happiness multiplies and blooms like a beautiful garden.

And then you're something like living as you should be.

As I said before, the happier you make people, the happier you become yourself. Oneness is the opposite of here. Here, anything you give away, you haven't got any more - whereas the giving of extensions of the Source, like love, happiness and joy, are then multiplied many times over.

I spoke about this once before, but it's always worth talking about it again. An aspect of Oneness is that giving is the same as receiving. This means that, whatever you do, whatever you give, you get back. It's got to come from your subconscious though. You can't ever do it for conscious gain. You could go and give someone a hundred dollars, and hope it will reflect back as a thousand dollars, but it doesn't work like that. However, if you give them your last hundred dollars, for example, to save them from something terrible... If you ever had the heart to do that - my God, what would the reflection be back on you then? It'd be something very, very wonderful, wouldn't it?

That's when you are really contacting Oneness. That's when you realize giving is the same as receiving. Therefore, having must be the same as being in the world of Oneness. It's all around us. We just can't see it. But every day, we're feeling it more and more. The vibe is intensifying, and it is a beautiful thing.

That's what I wanted to say. Two important aspects of Oneness: having is the same as being. And the second aspect: giving is the same as receiving. Just give love. Heartfelt, brotherly love and you can't go wrong. Your life will improve in a way you never thought possible. Truly.

# TRUTH CONNECTION NINETEEN: THE NON-EXISTENT FUTURE.

I'D like to say a few words about the future. In previous connections, I've spoken about the past in the sense of stopping thinking about the past. It is the past that causes us to be guilty and causes us a lot of problems that aren't necessary at all.

All we have to do, is stop thinking about the past. I know it's not easy to do that straightaway, but you can train yourself to do it. That is what I am doing, and doing very well at it. I just get happier and happier as each old guilty memory is dealt with and discarded. Bring Truth to the old memory. It is nothing but an illusion.

The future manufactures worry. Every time you think about the future, it brings about worry. The main trouble caused by future thinking is when people assume or presume things. For example, a loved one says they will be home by a certain time but they don't arrive. As each hour ticks by, we get more and more apprehensive and fret more and more until we're nearly tearing our hair out with worry. Your mind then starts going through its galleries and pictures and comes up with the most horrific things it can think of – the worst that it can find. It scares you half to death when really there is no evidence whatsoever that this is going to happen. It is only your memory of what happened at one time, or what you may have read about. There's no reason at all to think it is going to happen again, but notice your ego always takes you to those sort of images. It never takes you to images that say, "Oh, he (or she) is okay, nothing's happening there, I know where they'll be." It is always that negative, nagging worry. The thoughts keep nagging at you about this possible future, made up out of images from the past. It's a mixture of both. Never presume anything. How many times have you been wrong? You may have presumed something happened, or you may assume something is going to happen – yet it transpires that you've been completely wrong.

And what happens when you find out you've been wrong, which is about 99.9% of the time? You suffer terrible guilt.

You can't win with the past or the future. You've just got to stay in the now. It's all there really is.

# Truth Connection Twenty: The Extra Spiritual Mile.

Have a think about that saying, "If a brother asks you to walk a mile with him, go two". That makes a lot of sense. You know why? Because whatever you feel in your subconscious, is projected outwards and then reflected back at you.

Cultivate the kind of understanding that if a brother asks you to go a mile with him, or for you to help him in any way, that you'll go two with him, or help him the best you can with good heart.

For that's what will be projected out, and the world will do its best for you. It will walk two miles with you. This gives a whole (Holy) new meaning to the phrase.

# Truth Connection Twenty-One: Everybody is Everybody Else.

I'd like to say a word about our existence here as a dream... As an illusion... Or even an idea, you could call it. But it is an illusion, nonetheless. The best way to think of it, to make sense of it, is that it is a dream. And everybody in this dream, is you.

As you read this now, you are within my dream, just as I am within yours. So therefore, everybody you meet is in your dream, and everything you give to them, you give to yourself. No matter how fearsome and unlike you they may appear to be, they *are* you. They are an aspect of you that you don't like very much, and is hidden away. It might be only a tiny little aspect of you, but in your dream it grows to a great big aspect, doesn't it? Even so, it is just a dream. Everything you've done in it up until this present point doesn't matter in the grand scheme of things because it really is but a dream. All the details only remain in your head. It is the same for everybody else. They are all dreaming as well. If everybody forgot their past at some given signal, we would all stand completely equal, exactly as we are in the reality of Oneness. With no memory, we're One again, as we are in Reality. Of course, there are basic rules to survive here in this illusionary world. The thing to remember is, once you start feeling unhappy, you're thinking wrongly. Do your best to stop it immediately and get back on track. We're all on the road home, so why not make it as comfortable as possible?

# Truth Connection Twenty-Two: The Truth Has No Opposite - The Key to Understanding.

ONE of the greatest clues to the Truth of our real existence here, that this is a dream, an illusion, is the fact that Truth has no opposite. Everything here has an opposite. As I said before, every single color has an opposing color. We have male and female, black and white, back and front, side to side, good and evil; countless opposites.

All except one: Truth. Truth has no opposite.

Someone could say lies are an opposite to truth. But what are 'lies' but an empty nothingness? Some could say, 'Error', but what does error mean, except that something is not as it should be?

Just like everything around us is not as it should be. We're not Home.

Truth has no opposite and that is the greatest clue, because in the world of Oneness, where we come from, Oneness has no opposite. It can't have an opposite, otherwise it would not be

Oneness. Oneness literally means that. Simply Oneness. If it had an opposite, it would be twoness. But it's not, it's Oneness. Therefore, if it can't have an opposite, all of us, in our seemingly opposing existence here, can only be an illusion. A dream it is. That's the greatest clue of all. There are other clues, of course, but this is a really good one.

# Truth Connection Twenty-Three: Visions and the Illusionary Devil.

Here are some thoughts about the Source and His so-called opposite, the devil.

In Truth, the Source exists and the devil, in opposition, doesn't.

The devil isn't 'real'. He exists here in this illusion. His evidence is all around the world. You can read about the evidence of his being here in newspapers and on the TV news every day. Seeing as it is all a nightmare anyway, it doesn't really matter. You know those visions of St Joan seeing the Virgin Mary at Lourdes, and those at Fatima, etc? One interesting thing about those visions, is that everybody who sketched or drew the face of the Virgin Mary in those visions, sketched the face of a Western woman. Now bear in mind that not everybody saw this vision of the Virgin Mary. Not everybody in the crowd could see her; just a great many. They were in a kind of ecstasy. In their subconscious, being very religious, something triggered a mass projection to produce an image of the Virgin Mary outside of them and they could see it in adoration. Which is great...

except they were adoring a projection of their minds. Her appearing to be Western in the drawings, shows they were following an image of an icon, or even a Christmas card. In church icons and Christmas cards, the Virgin Mary always has a Western face, but she was from the Middle East, so she couldn't have had a Western face. This means they were not seeing the real Virgin Mary. What they were seeing is an image in their mind of what they think the Virgin Mary looks like, conjured up by icons and Christmas cards and the like. The same thing goes for the devil, and those that worship him. If enough of them get it into their heads that they want to see this be-horned, trident-bearing creature, he will appear for them. Then they will give him their worship and do any old stupid thing they think he's commanded them to do. But really, they're just worshipping nothing. Any wealth they may have accumulated for worshipping such an illusionary being, is just an illusional heap of snow. Spiritually barren, spiritually impoverished, but with great big piles of metal discs, little sheets of paper and lengthy rows of zeroes on a computer screen. Anything of material value in this world, is worth zilch in the spiritual world. This is because, just like our dreams at night, it isn't real. Not at all. There's only one Reality, and that's Oneness. The Source. And we're all going to get there. For some, however, it's going to take a little longer than others. But we're all going home. Fear not.

# Truth Connection Twenty-Four: Thank Heaven We're All Dreaming.

There is something everybody can do in times of stress, or when they are lonely or unwell - or in any kind of negative state. And that is to say to themselves, "I'm dreaming. Thank God I'm dreaming."

No matter how you feel about things, you can always say to yourself, "I am dreaming. Thank God I am dreaming." Or if you'd rather not talk about God - because I've noticed a lot of people don't like using the word 'God' - usually because it reminds them of religion, then say 'the Source' instead. The Source is what it is. The Source is an energy. A great, great energy. Certainly not a giant man standing on a cloud surrounded by angelic hosts.

Anyway, to say, or to remember, that you're dreaming, any time that you need it, is a very handy tool - especially when someone is angering you. Come to think of it, nobody really angers anybody; it's the angered one who has decided to be angry, but we'll talk about that another time. Realize you are dreaming.

It's like atheists and their like. They say they are non-believers, but when it comes to the nitty-gritty, they'll secretly say to themselves, "Oh God, help me out of this."

They suddenly become non-atheists. Not all of them, of course; but a great many. What I'm saying is, no matter how you feel about it, just think, "Thank God, I'm dreaming." Whether you really believe it or not, it helps just as much (or more) as suddenly turning to believing in God. And it helps, because it's true. You really are dreaming. A multi-purpose thought for any negative time.

# Truth Connection Twenty-Five: The Wholeness (Holiness) of Oneness.

This is a recap on an earlier connection concerning Oneness, time and space, and what they really are. First of all, Oneness is the opposite of here. Whereas here on earth, everything is separated, in Oneness it is exactly that, everything is One. It is unlimited, changeless, eternal and completely whole. Or holy, even. Holy, 'wholly'. Whole. Complete. As One.

The separation, or the illusion, which we're now inhabiting came about from an idea within the Oneness. Let's just say this is Oneness (put your palms together as if in prayer). Nothing is separated at all. It just goes on forever and ever and ever. We can't imagine it within our separated existence here, but that's what it is. Then within the Oneness, "Boom!" (pull your hands apart to demonstrate separation), as the idea of separation comes about.

Now, within the idea, there has to be space (like between your hands). Space comes about in order to demonstrate separation. To demonstrate that things are parted and viewable as separate items.

That's all space is.

Time is created as a by-product, because it takes time to cross space. We spend our entire lives going from A to B in one form or another. From the blood rushing round our veins, from a person walking over to a distant tree or whatever. It all takes time; and that time, this getting from A to B, is what we call our lives. And our lives, really, are what we do filling this getting from A to B. Literally trying to put back together where we come from. Brick by brick. But we can't really. It doesn't make sense. It is chaos as opposed to the perfect simplicity of Oneness. Just putting things back together gets us nowhere. We're simply trying to make sense of something that makes no sense at all.

# TRUTH CONNECTION TWENTY-SIX: WE ARE WHOLLY (HOLY) SPIRIT.

WHEN we think about ourselves, we see ourselves as being a body, rather than being the spirit we actually are. The body is just a vehicle. The brain itself doesn't think; the spirit uses it to think. It doesn't make any decisions; it is just a machine. The brain is just organic material. Every one of us is made of organic material. The body is made out of food. It is the same body we had when we were babies, except it now looks entirely different. Transformed by what? Food and drink. A bit further on, we look completely different again, but we're still the same being.

When you reach the age of 50, you say, "My God, I don't feel 50." That's because there never was a 'feeling 50.' When you're around 16 years of age, people of 50 seem so impossibly old, you think they must live in some different world or whatever. But when you get there, you find it's just the same, and you think, "Well, I don't feel 50," but there never was any feeling 50 to start with. The spirit seems to reach an acceptable age and just stay there. That's not a bad thing is it? The spirit never grows old; it is ageless. What I am saying is that we are spirit. We're not a body at all. That's why, when some people lose a limb, they say that they feel it is still there. They are feeling their spirit.

Really, we're not much more than vehicle. In a way, we're like cars going around with the driver sitting behind the wheel with his arms folded, waiting for the car to stop and think, "Wait a minute, I'm just a car - let's let the driver take over."

Indeed, we are something like that. Also, we are always having lots of accidents; just like cars crashing into each other and other general mayhem, like traffic jams. The body is just a vehicle. It doesn't do anything at all, except what you command it to do; it doesn't suddenly take itself off to the shop or dance about of its own accord. Like the computer - we use the computer to communicate, but it isn't part of us. And neither is the body. It's just a vehicle. And the brain is just a computer.

The Spirit is us. And it's all of us.

# Truth Connection Twenty-Seven: Notes on Awakening.

In this connection I want to discuss a few things about helping yourself to awaken. I'm well aware how hard it is not to interact with the illusion. I've been saying things like *don't think about the past* and *don't think about the future*. Which you shouldn't, but I know it's really hard not to. When you are sitting watching a film, you know the film isn't real, but you can get pretty involved in it, especially the emotional scenes. If you get so excited or involved watching a film or the TV, how are you going to stop yourself interacting with life? The only way to do that is to stop thinking. It can be done.

The spiritual teacher Eckhart Tolle advocates that you meditate and wait for gaps between the thoughts and then seize on that gap. In A Course in Miracles, it says you must wait for the Holy instant; well, not really wait for it, but seek it. The Holy instant is found the same way – in not thinking. As there is no future or past, you have to know it's already there. You have to know. That's the difference between Truth and this existence. Oneness is knowing; here is just thinking. When you know, you're Home. Stopping thinking is what meditation is. That's what those monks do up in the monasteries in Tibet. Sitting there not thinking - abandoning all judgment and seeing someone/something as if you've never seen him/it before. Connecting. And we can all do it. You not only stop yourself thinking negative thoughts, you try and stop thinking altogether. That's where the realm of Oneness is. If you stop thinking, you'll see the world as it Truly is. Not right away, because it's hard to stop thinking. But when you manage it, in that Holy Instant, the Source can then come in…

… and He will flood in.

And you'll wonder why you never saw Him before.

# Truth Connection Twenty-Eight:
# No Opposites = No Conflict.

Do you know, every single problem in the whole world, in the whole universe, is down to one thing?

Separation.

Which is what this illusion is all about. And everything being separated into perfect opposites. In the reality of Oneness, with it being changeless, endless, whole and unlimited - completely One - there's no such thing as problems.

Because in a world of no opposites, there's no conflict. If there's no conflict, there is only the perfect peace of Perfect Love.

It's as simple as that. It's the complexities of this world that makes the simplicity of Oneness so difficult to understand. That's why, when you ask people to stop thinking, they can't imagine that degree of not doing anything. They can't imagine their minds not doing anything. Many people go through their entire life thinking - and why should it ever occur to them not to do so? Thinking is an intrinsic part of our lives, so we think. And yes it is.

But our lives aren't real. We have to stop thinking to get to Reality. And Reality is no conflict at all. Everything is One. As I've said before, giving is the same as receiving; just as having is the same as being. There is no lack at all in Oneness. And we're all on our way there. Isn't that truly a great thought?

# TRUTH CONNECTION TWENTY-NINE: THE ILLUSIONARY WORLD OF LAUGHTER.

In this connection I want to say something about the illusion being a joke. What I mean by that is, once you see the illusion for what it really is, you see it for the joke it is.

When you think it's real, it's just not funny, is it? But once you realize it is not real, you begin to see it in a different light. It's like when someone tells you a joke. It's funny in itself, that. Someone can tell you the most horrible, disgusting and/or upsetting story, and at the end, you'll laugh your head off, because prior to telling it, they said the magic words, 'This is a joke'. Once those magic words have been said, he's then free to tell the most horrible story he can think of about all sorts of unsavory, ghastly subjects and the people in his audience are laughing themselves stupid.

Because it's a joke.

If you take away that phrase before he told the story, like a news report or something, the reaction would be very, very different. The illusion is a joke. And once you know it's a joke, it's really,

really funny. That's something to concentrate on. Life really is a dream. We have free will like the people in our dreams. We do what we like, just like the people in our dreams. And like the people in our dreams, when the dream's over, that's it. We just go home. Like the dream people, we are re-absorbed back into the Source. Before that happens, get realizing this is a dream—and get happy. See the joke. It is a really funny one.

# Truth Connection Thirty: The True Nature of Forgiveness.

This connection concerns the True nature of forgiveness, and how to apply it. As I said in an earlier discussion, True forgiveness is about realizing that the whole world is an illusion and that nobody in it has actually done anything. Like the people in your dreams at night, no matter what crimes they may appear to commit in your dreams, when you awake they are just nothing.

As this world is an illusion, everything that goes on here is an illusion too and you forgive it by realizing that. No matter what happens here, it is nothing but an illusion.

I don't mean freely forgive people for terrible murders, nothing like that. You have to consider the people who are still here thinking it is 'real'. Once you realize it is all an illusion, you feel a kind of duty to let people know.

When you look at all the world's agonies you realize that people are suffering for nothing. They think the dream is real. They think that the nightmare is real. They are interacting with it and suffering terribly. You have to enlighten them.

You realize that if you haven't forgiven everybody and you're getting angry, you are just the same as them. You can't teach them unless you are healed yourself. So, you begin by forgiving them.

This tip from the great Louise L. Hay is an excellent method of all-purpose forgiveness. She cured herself of cancer by starting off this way, as I understand it. Every time she felt any anger against anybody, she just said to them in her mind, "I forgive you for not doing what I wanted you to do." Really, all anger is induced by people not doing what others wanted them to do. And why should they? If you stop getting angry because they won't do what you want them to do, the problem is solved there and then. If you can apply this every time you get angry with anybody or irked in any way, even in the slightest, realize that you're getting irked because they are not doing what you want them to do. Forgive them for it. Once you can apply that kind of forgiveness, like Louise curing her cancer, you really start getting somewhere.

# Truth Connection Thirty-One: The Road to Awakening.

This connection concerns the three main rules of ACIM, which are stated pretty close to the beginning of the Course.

The first one: *'To have, give all to all'*. This is referring to projection. You give to receive. The more you give, the more you get back, but we're talking about things like love, happiness and joy. Not money and stuff like that. If you give money to somebody and it aids them to have happiness, then that happiness will reflect back on you.

The second one: *'To have peace, teach it'*. It's the same thing. If you teach peace, it's going to reflect back on you. That's how you have peace. If you are peaceful with everybody, everybody is peaceful with you. After all, who is unkind to a kind man?

And the last one: *'Be vigilant for God'*. This means look out for those negative thoughts. If you feel yourself starting to feel unhappy, anxious or guilty in any way, stop them. Get some positive ones on board. Or best of all, stop thinking at all. These are three good, solid foundation stones on the road to awakening.

Stick with ACIM's three rules and you can't go wrong. I won't say good luck because you won't need it. It's there for you.

# Truth Connection Thirty-Two: Think Yourself Awake.

A lot of people have asked me the question, "How do you absorb this knowledge?" The mere act of reading the information in ACIM, doesn't mean to say that you instantly take it all in. At least it's a start though.

Knowledge is a start. Once you've absorbed everything it tells you, then you have to keep pondering on it; thinking about it all the time until it becomes your normal way of thinking.

Once it has become your normal way of thinking, then obviously it seems normal. It becomes an everyday thing to know that this is an illusion. And that's a great relief.

During the Second World War, Nazi Propaganda Minister Joseph Goebbels was reputed to have said, "If you tell a lie big enough and keep repeating it, people will eventually come to believe it."

It will never, however, become an actual truth. However, this works in reverse too.

If you tell yourself the Truth long enough and often enough, the Truth sinks in. Then, once the Truth has sunk in, you know everything is an illusion and your road to awakening then becomes much, much firmer.

# TRUTH CONNECTION THIRTY-THREE: BEGINNINGS AND ENDINGS.

Here's an interesting experiment. Ask someone if they can speak Chinese (or any language that you know they cannot speak). When they say 'no', as they probably will (unless you ask a Chinese person), you then ask, "When did your ignorance of Chinese begin?" They are going to respond along the lines of, "What are you talking about? I've never known Chinese. Never, ever. If I don't know Chinese, how can I have ever known Chinese?"

So you say, "Well, if you decide to learn Chinese, then your ignorance of Chinese will come to an end." Therefore, what has no beginning, has an end. How can something that has no beginning, that never was there, have an end? There must be a beginning, because in this world of opposites, if there's an end, there must have been a beginning. If there's cause, there's effect. If there's effect, there must have been a cause.

So where was this beginning of not being able to know Chinese?

It was at the beginning of the dream; the beginning of what you could call creation. The creation of the dream when everything separated and we forgot who we were. And we forgot how to speak Chinese.

Not necessarily Chinese, but we're from Oneness, where everything is One – including Chinese. It is part of the Oneness. It is everything. That's where learning Chinese was lost; when the dream began. And once it had a beginning. It had to have an end.

# Truth Connection Thirty-Four: The Snake in the Shed.

There's one thing definite about wandering around the Australian bush, beautiful though it is - there are lots of creatures in it, including many types of snakes. Kangaroos, bandicoots, numbats, lots of lizards and the afore-mentioned snakes, though you don't often come across them. If you tread warily, stamp loudly as you walk, the snakes are likely to just slither off. This reminds me about the story of the Indian guy who goes to his shed to get a spade.

He goes there at dusk and as he opens the door, in the darkness he sees a huge snake curled up on the floor. After his initial shock, he goes rushing off to get his neighbours to help him get the snake out of his shed. They all come back by torchlight, armed with clubs and stuff to sort out this snake. When they get there, they throw open the door, cast their torches round the shed, and find that the 'snake' is actually just a big coil of rope.

What a mistake, but also what a relief.

Do you know what this whole world is? That 'snake' on that piece of rope. All the fears we have in the world are just like that image of that snake cast on that coil of rope. They aren't really there. We just think they are. There's no 'snake' at all.

# Truth Connection Thirty-Five: On Origin of Existence.

When a person looks at things like animal skulls, that of a kangaroo, for instance, they absolutely marvel. All the little holes in it make it very lightweight. The teeth immaculately made. Everything superbly designed to be the perfect skull for a kangaroo, or whatever.

But who could have designed it, if that was the case? If it was designed, then that means that there was someone before him, who would have needed designing himself. So that means the designer idea can't be right, can it? If we ask, 'How did we get here?' and are answered, "Someone designed it and that's how we all got here," that indicates there was something before that, so it can't be a beginning.

No. All that happened was... We started to dream... There was nothing before our lives. There was nothing before my life. When I was born, I began gathering information from ongoing experiences and events around me, until I became what I am now. How did the skull get so intricate? Because it was created by a perfect mind. The same perfect mind that created us. In that perfect mind, everything is done perfectly. When the idea of separation came, it was carried out perfectly; everything you see is perfect within a world of separation. It's even more perfect back Home though. Because there is Perfect Love. And that's all we really need.

All we Truly Are.

# Truth Connection Thirty-six: Animals - A Reflection of Ourselves.

I'VE had a few people ask, "What about animals? Does it say anything about them in ACIM?" Well, it mentions them a few times, but to me, animals are an expression of ourselves.

We see animals as we project ourselves onto them. If we see animals as loving, then we're generally loving ourselves. If we don't like animals, then the animals don't like us. You get people who say, "Oh, I don't like animals - they don't like me." Of course they don't – it's because you don't like them. It's a reflection. Everything is a reflection. If you're full of love, it reflects onto everything.

When I was a little boy, I loved animals. I really loved them and I've never forgotten that love for them. However, I lost my inclination to keep them. I never had a cat or a dog in adulthood. I still liked animals, but I lost that wanting to have one near me, wanting to have one with me. When I saw through the illusion and got rid of all my negative stuff, I started to love animals again.

This is because I started to project it. A love for everything is reflected back at you. You do get the odd tweak, the odd gremlin in it, but you are in a world of illusions. You can't escape it completely.

However, they just get smaller and smaller, until you barely notice them. And you can handle that, can't you? How you see animals is how you see yourself. See yourself as beautiful and you'll see them that way too. Because they are.

# Truth Connection Thirty-Seven: Science and the Illusion.

I was just thinking about science and its eternal quest to find out what this is all about. Fascinating stuff, but within an illusion, how can a person ever prove for sure, that their information is correct? They draw their conclusions. They write up their formulas. But it seems like the information in it is only knowable to their own little club. I mean, science is great, and it's really interesting - but really, it's just an investigation of something that isn't real.

The philosopher, Karl Popper, observed that all Science theory, no matter what it concerns, cannot be proved 100% correct, but it will always be susceptible to the possibility of being proved wrong to some degree.

I had a dream once, that I was looking out across a large, stark wasteland, and coming across this wasteland was a strange little creature – or half-man, half-creature. It was like nothing I've ever seen before. It had two eyes like tennis balls, the most peculiar spinning arms, its locomotion was so bizarre, I woke up thinking seriously, "What was that?" This happened about 20 years ago, or perhaps even longer, but it doesn't matter. I was so impressed with this dream that I got a piece of paper and a pen and drew this creature, because I'd never seen anything like it before and it was in my dream. I've never seen anything like it since. So what was this creature? He was entirely my creation. There's nothing like him here.

He had a very strange method of locomotion that I can't really explain here. If I wanted to find out how he moved, seeing as he was my creation, I'd have to somehow get back inside my dream and track him down. Perhaps like a good inquisitive scientist I'd have to then knock him out and cut him open to see what was inside to see how he functioned; to find out how this creature worked; to know all about him. The thing is though, no matter what I found inside him, it would still be a dream, wouldn't it? All the conclusions I drew, would also be a dream. Just like here. Science is fun, but it's still just a dream.

# Truth Connection Thirty-Eight: No Past = Best Future.

I would like to say a bit more about our existence here being like a stage, and us being players on it. All the scenery is supplied.... All the props.... Except we write our own scripts while we're here.

The trouble with most relationships, is that our past comes into the relationship with us and people judge other people by their past. Their perceptions of each other are totally wrong, because each of them are not talking to the real person, so to speak, only but a past version.

Underneath, we're all the same being, and that's what we have to get in contact with. When you meet your special partner, or someone you want to remain with long term, the only way to make it work is to forget your past. Both of you have to do this, and start again. Start again with no thought for the future and no regard for the past. It can only but work, can't it? As it is right now, each one of us appears on the earth, walks onto the stage, so to speak, and starts writing his script, hanging labels on all that's around him. He starts deciding the personalities and whims and idiosyncrasies of people he meets. Put that all together, and that's his life. The stories his partner or friend tell him, he puts together to make what he thinks is their life. He decides where it matches up with his. Where it doesn't match up, it all goes wrong and they start arguing, and stuff like that. Forgetting each other's past is the only way when you think about it; then you both get home together.

# Truth Connection Thirty-Nine: Prayer That Works and Finding the Source.

A lot of people think the Source, or God, is hidden out there in the distance somewhere. Somewhere around us. Not within. Well, I think that anybody who has come this far with this small tome is aware that God is within us now. We try desperately to find Him. We pray for Him to come and help us out. Pray for him to come and do this or that, or pray to him to provide something we haven't got. When really, we've all been praying to him wrongly in the first place.

True prayer is understanding that the Source, or God, is in the present, the eternal present. Oneness is eternal and it is eternally present. And He is in it. We can't see it, but its here. So when you pray for things, you tell the Source that you've already got it. After all, you're the one who is having this dream. When you pray for things, you tell the Source that you've already got it.

Then the universe or the Source, or the material universe, will turn the great wheels of the illusion to bring it into your present. Asking for things in the future, suggests want in the present. Because the Source only understands the present, a state of want is what you are kept in. God is within. That's why you ask within. Well, you don't actually ask, you just tell Him. "I've got this car", or whatever it is you want. However, I'd advise not to ask for cars and/or similar. Just blanket cover it by asking for happiness. He knows what makes you happy. Simply ask to be happy. That's all you need. God is looking for us. All this stuff about we've got to do this, and we've got to do that and we've got to pray and one day He will come - one day He will hear our prayer. In Truth, He is desperately trying to find us like any father would look for a lost son. The reason why He hasn't found us, or a great many of us, is because He is blocked off. He doesn't understand negativity. It's not in His world. His world has no opposites, It is just perfect love. Once we get rid of thinking, that's where He can be found. The good side of this existence leans towards Him, whereas the so-called bad side leans away from Him. Obviously, anything loving leans towards Him and anything that isn't, leans away. The closer you are to loving, the closer you are to Him. In fact, as the mystic and poet Rumi said, 'He is nearer than your jugular'. He is you. By thinking only loving thoughts He will come in. And once He's in, He's in for good.

# Truth Connection Forty: Living in the Past - Our Lives Were Over Long Ago.

I want to tell you a tale a Buddhist told me once. It concerns a Buddhist monk who lived in a village. A teenage girl in this village got herself pregnant by her boyfriend, and afraid of outraging her parents and the entire village, as was the moral code of the time when this story was about, she blamed it all on the Buddhist monk and said it was him; that he had raped her; that the baby was his. So of course, all the sympathy was on her side. When the baby was born, they all marched down to the Buddhist monk's house, banged on his door and said, "This is your baby, you made this girl pregnant." The monk replied, "Is that so?" then he took the baby, went into his house and shut the door. They are all looking round, thinking, "What the hell...?" But there was nothing they could do. They'd said the baby was his and he'd taken it and shut the door.

When the dust had settled a few months later, the girl and her boyfriend decided to get married. And when they decided that, they wanted their baby back. So they went back to see the Buddhist monk, somewhat shamefacedly, and knocked on his door. The monk opened it and said, "Yes?"

They said they were sorry they had blamed all their problems on him and explained that the boyfriend was the baby's father. The monk said simply, "Is that so?" and gave them the baby back and shut the door.

And that's the end of the story. When I was told that tale, I liked that story, although I wasn't quite sure why. I didn't quite get the meaning of it to begin with. But I realize now that the Buddhist monk was wise enough to know that this is what is known as 'dharma,' the eternal law of the cosmos. Whatever happens in this life has already passed; has already happened. The dream was over long ago. Because the dream happened in a timeless environment, it was over and done with in an instant. As I've explained before, time and space are here to demonstrate that everything is separated and because of them, we imagine it is ongoing and ongoing for billions of years, when in fact, that is only an illusion caused by time and space. The dream was over long ago. This means our lives were over long ago and whatever lies ahead of us, is already there. That's dharma, as I understand it. Can you change it? Of course you can change it, but in the end it will still be the same result, because way, way back, when the dream first appeared, you changed it then. Now, you're still in the process of doing it. Because you are within the dream. But the dream is over.

The enlightened Advaita master Ramesh Balsekar often used the metaphor that life is like a painting (Wayne Liquorman described it as a fifty-mile long painting)

This painting is so huge, a person can only see one section of it at a time. Let us imagine I am standing in a forest and this forest is part of this painting. I can only see one part at a time as I walk along the fifty miles observing this huge work of art. As I go past, no matter what the painting is about, each section would blend in with what was coming next; I would see it as blending in with the features further along. When I got to the end of the painting fifty miles later, I'd have forgotten lots of the bits and pieces I'd passed, although I'd still have a rough idea of what the painting was generally about. And yet, when it is all said and done, it was still only a fifty-mile painting and if I'd stood far enough back, I'd have seen it happening all at once. And happening all at once, is how our existence came about all that time ago. Right now we're walking along that celestial fifty-mile painting we call life. We've done it all before.

And don't worry about it. It all turns out alright in the end.

# Truth Connection Forty-One: Effective Self-Forgiveness.

One of the hardest points of forgiveness is that of forgiving ourselves. We feel that our 'crimes' really are the worst of all. Forgiveness is all about realizing our 'crimes' and everybody else's are nothing but an illusion.

Or dream.

Or idea.

That nobody has actually done anything at all. ..

...and this includes yourself.

You haven't done anything at all. As every instant moves into the past, where is it now, except in your memory? Where you do what you want with it and you terrify yourself with it. You can twist it into whatever you want. You can make whatever you want with your memories. You really can. But be sure of one thing, they are not real.

Not a single one of them.

So forgive yourself – no matter how terrible that memory may be - because it's only a dream.

Within the illusion, if you've done something as socially unacceptable as murdering somebody for example, within the illusion, it is not an acceptable action for obvious reasons. But in a nightmare, it's just something that happened in a nightmare.

And we're in that nightmare. Oh yes, and don't we all know it.

But that's all it is. A bad, bad dream. Forgive yourself.

Start from this instant NOW. This very instant.

Forgive yourself for all that's gone before and start again. Start again this very instant. For you and everybody else.

As a bonus, imagine that everybody else is forgiving everything in the same instant that you choose to do it. Don't worry about whether or not they are actually doing so.

For an instant, forget everything. And start again. If you can't do it that instant, try the next instant. Or maybe the next instant or five minutes from that.

But keep trying. It's one of the best routes to enlightenment. The best way to forgive yourself.

# Truth Connection Forty-Two: Spirit and Indestructible Water.

I once read that with all the water on the planet - I don't know exactly how much that is, but obviously it's billions of tons of water - the amount of it never changes.

It can't go anywhere, can it? The amount of water that's here is the same amount of water that was here at the beginning of the planet. Or the beginning of the dream, if you like. The same water the dinosaurs drank.

The amount of water never changes. It's always here. Every single drop of rain is part of that great body of water. It never loses a drop. Never gains a drop. It's always the same. I also read about an Indian swami, who compared us to bottles. Lots of different colored bottles, all different shapes and sizes. Some with nice corks. Some with fancy tin hats. Some with labels. Some without.

Just a lot of old bottles, or new bottles.

Thousands of assorted bottles.

And they all hold water.

Line each of them up and then walk along looking at them all. Marveling at their sheer diversity.

And then one falls on the floor, and the bottle's no more. The water runs out from the shattered bottle. It evaporates and goes back to join the never-changing amount of water that's always here. In fact, it doesn't matter what shape or color, or what cap, these bottles have, the water inside them is always the same. You can't get rid of it. If you smashed all the bottles, you're still left with all the water. And no matter what you do with it, it eventually re-joins the original amount. Be it ice, liquid or steam. Mysterious water - and really, it's just the same as us. Water, when you think about it, is an example of us in Spirit. Indestructible, and it can take on many forms.

Bottles come and bottles go, but only the water is 'real'. And it the long run, even water is not Truly 'real'. It's just part of the dream. A very interesting part.

# Truth Connection Forty-Three: The Illusion and Indestructible Gold - and a Spider.

Another thing we could metaphorically align ourselves with is gold. By 'ourselves,' I mean our spirit; the Oneness of our spirit. Gold is perceived to be indestructible. I suppose if you vaporized it, it would be broken down to molecular level, but all those molecules are still gold molecules. They still take up the same space collectively, so to speak, but that's another subject.

Now if we've got a gold ring, we think of it intrinsically as a ring. Decoration. A token of love or worth. But anyhow, it's a ring. We think of it as a ring.

Then one day someone decides to melt it down and make a thimble out of it. Well, now it's a thimble and has a totally different use. However, the gold itself isn't even aware it has changed shape. It's just a piece of gold. Forever beautiful as gold ever is. No matter what you do with it, and no matter how small you break it down, it's always there. No matter what you make out of it. Just like the dream we're in, it's all made out of the same stuff. It's all made out of the Source. Look around you at the different things you can make out of it.

Astonishing, isn't it?

Just as water is indestructible, gold is another example. There's lots of them here. Another one is a spider. He creates his own little world out of himself and uses it to survive. Yes, there's lots of little things here. It's great fun looking out for them.

# Truth Connection Forty-Four: Thoughts on our Spiritual Evolution.

Regarding the ongoing spiritual evolution, it seems to me like the people of the earth, or very much the larger proportion, have all been very much like children going to see a conjuring act. Like a child going to see a magician's show with his adult parents. They look up on the stage and see the magician pulling rabbits out of a hat and sawing a woman in half and doing all sorts of things that seem impossible. To a child, his tricks will indeed seem magic. When you're a child, you wouldn't understand any kind of sleight of hand, or trickery. Things are as you see them. It is a magical world for young children. The adult sitting with him still sees the same tricks, but he knows they're an illusion. He may not know how the magician does these tricks, but it doesn't matter, because he still knows it's an illusion. In fact, no matter what trick this magician may perform, the adult knows that however amazing it is, it *must* still be an illusion.

What I'm saying is, the children at the magician's show are just like the people on earth. The adults, or knowledgeable ones, sitting there with them, knowing it is all an illusion, have been, up until now, just a very few. However, the real great news is that the spiritual evolution is going on apace and a great many of those people who once thought the tricks were real, are not being fooled any more. Isn't that really something?

We're getting there.

# Truth Connection Forty-Five: Retaining Inner Peace - Deflecting Projected Anger.

Anger is a decision. Everything is a decision here. All day long we go through decisions - shall I turn left, shall I turn right? Shall I pick this up - shall I not pick it up? Shall I ignore this or shall I not?

Just one decision after another.

A judgment - shall I, shan't I?

It's only here in this existence because in Oneness, our home, there's nothing to choose from. Everything's there, in complete wholeness (Holiness).

Regarding anger. Even if someone is screaming and yelling in your face, he's not really annoying you, it's you who are deciding to be annoyed about it. No matter how intense the provocation.

You can decide not to be annoyed about it.

Not the easiest option to take and could well be very hard to accomplish, but once all the screaming and shouting has died down, he's left feeling foolish and you're left feeling cool, calm and collected.

And you can walk away from this argument that never was, unharmed, unhurt, un-pained.

Because you refused to argue. Refused to be negative. Refused to take the reflection. That is what that person who is shouting and screaming at you is doing – looking closely for his reflection. If you display the slightest twitch of an eyelid, or any little sign to show that you're reflecting his anger back, then he will 'go to town'. His anger is then unleashed and you've accepted it and any perceived little spark of it shows that he's rooted it in you and he will go into emotional overdrive and you will find yourself fighting back, if only in a tiny way.

Even if you don't argue back, once you've accepted his anger, you will become pained. You might think as you wander off, "Why didn't I give it to him, why didn't I really tell him? Why didn't I tell him what I thought of him?"

You think such stuff because you accepted that anger. Even though you accepted just a tiny little bit, it's enough to make you pained and hurt.

Don't accept any of it. I'm not saying give in to his argument. I'm saying, at the end, you could say, "Well, here's what I think," and all they can do then, is listen, because the argument they thought they were going to have hasn't happened and there you stand rational, calm and collected. Seeing as they haven't been able to project it and have it reflected back, the anger stays with them, and all it can do is subside. That's their problem. This is your dream and we're worrying about you right now. Don't accept that anger. It makes for a lot easier life. Hard work mind, initially, as you learn to apply this thinking; but remember, it's your choice. Don't accept that anger. If you don't want it, don't accept it. Be happy. It's there for you.

# Truth Connection Forty-Six: ACIM - Gaining Control of the Mind.

In this connection I want to talk about ACIM, or A Course in Miracles, as a mind-training course. Which in fact, it is. A course in training your mind to reverse its thinking processes, i.e. thinking this is real becomes reversed into knowing it is not 'real'. Then you can start enjoying yourself. If you're in the middle of a nightmare, in a night time dream, and you awaken within the dream and realize that you are dreaming, you're not afraid any more, are you? You see it for what it is and then you can have some fun because you know it can't hurt you. You know that it is just a dream. That's what ACIM is. It trains your mind to realize this is just a dream.

Of course, being here, our egos interact with the dream all the time because the ego relies on the dream for its existence. We aren't real. We just think we're real. These constant barrages of guilt that most of us get thrown at us all the time, is the ego tormenting us. Whatever you think of, whatever subject you are thinking about, do you notice the ego can find some linking subject; some cringe-worthy or guilt-ridden thought that'll come and torment you? It does that all the time. It always finds something to connect. Well, the Course trains you to get the ego out of your mind.

You can call it the devil if you like, because it torments you. It keeps you in your own little hell. The way out is to get the ego out, to drive it from your mind in order to get rid of those guilty thoughts. It doesn't matter how you do it. It doesn't matter if you dwell on them, think about them, turn them over, decide they were actually good thoughts or whatever you want to do with them. Endeavor to reach the point where you can cast them from your mind and throw them away. What is essential is that you get them out of your mind. That is the only way to find inner peace.

Inner peace is what we're looking for. Inner peace is happiness.

You won't find inner peace with lots of guilty thoughts piled up on top of your table. You need to get rid of them. One way that I've found very helpful, is what I call the FODD method.

F for forgiveness

O for overlook

D for dismiss

D for disappear

As soon as one of these thoughts hit your mind, utilise 'F', forgive it. Then 'O' - overlook it - because it's just an illusion. Overlook it and then 'D' for dismiss it. Then on a click of your fingers (this seems to give added power), force it from your mind, and it will 'D' for disappear. Use that word 'FODD' and just blanket the thought. Hold it there until something more palatable comes floating by. Any thought that isn't giving you pain, or hurting you or worrying you, or causing you distress, is fine. It's the ones that hurt you that you don't want.

A more advanced method is to invite the Holy Spirit to observe the painful memory with you. To bring His Truth to it. As you both watch, His presence will cause it to dissolve and fade away; usually for good. If it comes back, invite Him again. Invite Him as often as needed. He won't mind. He is here with us right now for just such a purpose.

What we all could do with is loving thoughts all the time, and then you can't help but feel good all the time. What better or more satisfying goal could there possibly be?

## Truth Connection Forty-Seven: The Return of Oneness.

We only ever give to ourselves.

We are all individuals having the same dream. We are all of the same mind, split into a billion, if you like, individuals, all dreaming that they are individuals having individual lives. Fleshing it out with experiences and events that they go through as they grow up until reaching their present age, and believing it all to be 'real'.

As we're all having the same dream, each one of us can wake up and awaken all the rest.

Now, obviously one awakened person can't meet all the people in the world, so there has to be lots of awakening people all around the world, as there is right now, I'm very pleased to see. Realizing that, in this dream, everybody is you, goes a long way in getting things in perspective.

How you view things is the life you've decided for yourself. Change your views, change your life. Look at that person you hate. No, 'hate' is a horrible word; that person you may dislike. There's lots of people out there, including people we think we have great reason to dislike or even hate (notice that I said, 'we think' - it is all about *thinking*). Either stop thinking or change your thinking. Going back to everybody being you, you're the dreamer and this is your dream and everybody in it, is you. So whatever you do to them, you do to yourself. The nice things you want to do to your brothers and sisters, deep in your subconscious, will be projected out of you and will create scenarios around you of great love for you. And that great growing love for you and your brothers and sisters, is the return of Oneness. It is well on its way.

# Truth Connection Forty-Eight: Spirit Guidance and the True Path.

I want to say something about spirit guides, or spiritual guidance. If you want True spiritual guidance, you've got to forget any plans you've got, because they don't cater for careers or vocations. All they cater for is getting you Home.

Now, as I said before, this life of ours was over and done with millennia ago. It is time and space that create the illusion of years and minutes, seconds, months and weeks. It is entirely an illusion. There is no time. Time and space make us think we have lives, but it was over and done with in an instant, because it was created in a timeless environment - the Oneness we originate from. Those extensions of the Source that remain outside our environment can see our predicament and because they can see it from beginning to end, they can see all the obstacles that are in our way. If we manage to stop thinking, which is interacting with the illusion, they can aid us by putting before us scenarios and/or situations that benefit us if we decide wisely or positively.

That is guidance. Making the best of what comes before you. Don't think about it, because to think is to project, and that brings about your own destiny. We don't want our own destiny. We want our True destiny. When I say 'our own destiny', I mean one we imagine we've got, like success is owning your own house or whatever.

Of course it isn't.

Never mind about that.

Success is getting Home and these guides can see our whole journey from beginning to end. They can see the way around every obstacle and problem you will ever encounter on our way. So stop thinking ahead, stop planning, and just take life as it comes. Take it positively. Only think loving thoughts. So that only love is projected and only love is around you. That's true. It really is. Ask those guides and stop worrying. They'll take you where you need to be.

Where we all need to be.

# Truth Connection Forty-Nine: A Brief Word on Reincarnation.

It has come to my attention that a lot of people want to know about reincarnation. I haven't mentioned it before, because in A Course in Miracles, it says that any ideas of reincarnation, be it so or not so, are part of the illusion and it is pointless to discuss it as 'real'. An illusion is just an illusion. It certainly would appear that people have thousands and thousands of lifetimes. Some folk believe they are repaying old debts in this lifetime for crimes committed in their past ones.

But really, what would be the point of that if you can't remember what the crime was? No, reincarnation is just part of the dream. It would appear lots of things over many lifetimes happen to most people before they eventually get Home, but once you awaken and realize the Truth, you can't be reborn on earth any more. Unless, possibly, you want to be. Once you are aware it is just a dream, you awaken to True Reality.

Reincarnation may well be so, and it probably is. But it's all just part of the illusion, and like that illusion, there's no Truth to it.

# Truth Connection Fifty: Us, the Sons of God.

This is to recap on earlier connections that state that we are all sons of God. This thing about being the Son of God throws a lot of people, because they think Jesus was the Son of God. So how can they be the Son of God?

How can they be that powerful?

How can they be *that* kind of person? A Jesus Christ kind of person. How can that be me?

Look at it this way. We're in an illusion. We've established that. A dream.

Now the dream is more or less exactly the same as our dreams at night. It works on the same principle. Therefore, everybody in our dreams are the sons of us, so to speak. Men or women, they're our sons, technically, so everybody is the son of God in the same way that everybody in our night time dreams are the 'sons' of us.

Everything, every single thing, is us in our night time dreams, and every single thing I'm looking at now is God. Or the Source. Or whatever you want to call it. He's the only real there is. Although the world is just an illusion, it is made out of Him. Because we're using His power to produce it. Us, His Sons.

# Truth Connection Fifty-One: Naming the Nameless (Within a Forest).

I want to talk about the early lessons in A Course in Miracles, from one to five; where the Author discusses disconnecting yourself from the illusion, by first of all looking at each thing around you, and saying, "That grass there is meaningless. That gum tree is meaningless. The sky is meaningless. The ground is meaningless. This hat is meaningless. This arm is meaningless. This hand is meaningless." You apply this to anything in your vision.

Everything is meaningless. Absolutely everything. Then you realize that any meaning it has for you, is what you have given to it, including the names given to the various objects in view - well, perhaps you haven't named them yourself, but someone has told you what they are called.

I know the names of every single thing here. Everything here I could put a name on it or some name which I could recognize it by. And they are all applied to it by me on advice given. In Reality, they are none of those things; names and titles give things more solidity than they actually have.

I call a tree, 'a tree,' in order to talk to other people about it, e.g. "I saw this certain type of tree." But really, the name 'tree' gives it much more body than it actually has. It is just something in a dream, as is everything. Every single thing here I've named and when I am not here, it is nameless. An empty stage. Just waiting for me to come by and put names to it all, and to the illusion itself. None of it means anything at all.

# Truth Connection Fifty-Two:
# Glimpses of Truth - Tears of Sadness and Joy.

Have you ever wondered why people cry when they watch sad films? Or maybe something on the television? Or read a sad story? It's almost always about loss.

They're crying about the loss of a loved one, even though it isn't their loved one. Just the very idea of it is enough to reduce people to tears. It is a very, very hard man who doesn't shed a tear over somebody's death or the death of a pet even. But what are they actually crying about?

Becoming separated.

Again.

That's what they are crying about. It isn't just crying about loss, they're crying about reconciliation as well. When they see someone reconciled with a loved one on film or TV, whether it's in drama or actually really happening, people will cry and enjoy doing so, in some ways.

They're crying for Home, unwittingly. They're seeing a love that we've lost. They're seeing reconciliation. Something we've yearned for. When someone passes on, or becomes separate from us, they haven't really, but in this world of separation we think they have and we become very negative about it, as is this world. We think we've lost them, when in fact, we haven't at all. They've just left the dream. They're always here. There is only us. There is only Oneness. There is only the Source. And we are the Source. We yearn for our Source. And one day, we're going to find it.

All of us.

We recognize it in every sad film we see, and one day we will return to it. Every single one of us.

# Truth Connection Fifty-Three: The Creation of the Illusion.

I want to say something here about creation. Within this world, nothing is created. What is already here is created. We don't create anything. We just make things. We take bits of creation and put it together to make things. Creation is of the Source. We spoke previously about the design theory - how it can't be so, because if something has been designed, it follows that there must be something prior to that in order to have designed it. The design, therefore, cannot be a beginning. So creation - this - was just created.

By a perfect mind.

You can do it yourself. Think about anything and there it is. Think about it again and there it is again. Think about as many things as you want and they just appear in your mind, don't they?

Invent something new right now. Simply visualize it. Have a supernova in your mind and there it is. It just appears and it's there. That's how the Source works. It just appears and it's there. Like we appeared one day in the Source's dream about separation. Or *our* dream. But then again, we are the Source. And this is just a dream.

## Truth Connections

We're all awakening. Some quickly, some slowly. Have no doubt. We all get there in the end.

# Truth Connection Fifty-Four: How the Illusion Appears to be 'Real'.

People ask me, "How can this existence be an illusion? Everything feels real, everything is solid. You can pick something up, drop it and it will fall and smash on the pavement or whatever. How can it be a dream?"

When you are dreaming, the characters in your dream can pick up cups and do all kinds of other stuff, can't they? Just like you. Take a cartoon character like Bart Simpson. He picks up his cartoon cup and drinks out of it, but it isn't a real cup. He's a cartoon character and he's in the cartoon. Similarly, we are dream characters and we are in the dream. You pick up a cup in the dream, our existence here, and drink out of it and it feels solid and real because we feel solid and real. As with Bart Simpson, in the cartoon he is solid and real within his environment, just as we feel solid and real within our environment. We aren't much more than dream characters. We are just projected images. It is only ourselves that apply any meaning to it all.

# Truth Connection Fifty-Five: True Awakening - Seeing Through the Illusion.

A word about true awakening. True awakening is recognizing your brother, or yourself, in someone else.

Because you are everybody else.

As I've said before, we are dreaming and everybody in the dream is us. In my dream, everybody in it is me. For me to awaken from this dream, I have to recognize this. I have to recognize that everybody is my brother. I have to look beyond what I see with my illusional eyes, because my illusionary eyes can only see illusions. They are part of this 3-dimensional machine, which is actually a vehicle that I utilize to get me through this illusion. It is not true vision. True vision is of the mind and it can be found by your mind recognizing that your brother's mind is the same one as yours.

We are One.

As you become more and more positive in your thinking, you begin to realize that you are not meeting negative people any more. You are not meeting angry people any more. You are not meeting people who upset you anymore. Or if you are, you're meeting them in fewer number. There comes a time where you barely meet any negative people at all. If there is no negativity projecting out of you, there is none of it appearing around you. That is the true road towards awakening and seeing that everyone around you is your brother. He is you. We are One. And we're recognizing it big time now. These are great times. Every one of us is a brother. Once we recognize the dream is over we will fully realize this.

After all, at the end of every play, we applaud the villains as well as the heroes, do we not?

# Truth Connection Fifty-Six: ACIM Lesson 311. I Judge All Things as I Would Have Them Be.

Here, I'd like to attempt to simplify one of the Course's Lessons. As you know, there are 365 of them, one for every day of the year, but it's up to you how long you want to spend on each of them. The length of time doesn't matter, as long as you get there in the end.

Lesson 311: *'I judge all things as I would have them be'*. It starts off by saying judgment was made to be a weapon used against the Truth. This means that in Truth, which is Oneness, there cannot be any judgment. Oneness is one whole, unlimited never-ending thing. Actually, it is not even a 'thing.' A 'thing' indicates that it is separate from something else. It is not *any*thing. Nothing. No-thing. If there is only one thing, what is there to judge against? There is no judgment because Oneness says so. To judge, you have to judge one thing against another. If there's only one thing, there is nothing to judge against. So judging, or judgment, doesn't exist in Oneness.

That's how judgment is used against the Truth. If you judge something, e.g. "This is better than that," this is far removed from the Truth. In Oneness, nothing is better than anything else, as there is nothing else. The supposedly better one has been removed from Himself, so to speak.

Judgment separates what it is being used against and sets it off as if it were a thing apart. If you say I choose that thing over that thing because it is better, it is now a thing apart. "He's good and he's not so good." He becomes separated, enhancing the idea of separation. Judgment makes of a situation how you would have it be. For example, supposing you've been declared the winner, you then see yourself how YOU would have it to be. "I'm wonderful", "I'm hip", "I'm simply fantastic," or whatever you may care to think about yourself. That's making of it what you would have it to be. Judgment cannot see totality, therefore it judges falsely.

Any judgment made on me - that I am the winner, and I am therefore the best - is not judgment in totality. It's just *my* idea of it. I have no idea of the totality of the case to be judged. Regarding the person I've been judged better than, there must be someone in the world who thinks he is better than me. His mother, for example, would think this. Therefore I am not judging him in totality, because there are other people out there who see *him* as the winner. I'm not seeing the full picture so therefore the picture must be false. I must have judged falsely and all my images of me being a winner are just an illusion. In Reality, there is no judgment; we are all winners, so to speak.

The Lesson goes on to say, *'Let us not use it today, but make a gift of it to Him who has a different use for it.'* And further, *'He will relieve us of the agony of all the judgments we have made against ourselves, and re-establish peace of mind by giving us God's judgment of His son'*. This means that by giving judgment to Him, as in, "Okay God, you do the judging," we don't have to worry about it. It is our own judgment that has caused all the agony as a result of the judgments we have made against ourselves and all the suffering in the past. All that cringing and feeling guilty about judgments we made, that we now feel were wrong. We'll have none of that if we give Him judgment and he will judge us to be his son, because that is what we truly are within His/our dream.

The last part of the lesson, says, *'Father, we wait with open mind today to hear your judgment of the son you love'*. We are the son He loves and we are waiting for His judgment. *'We do not know him and we cannot judge.'* I don't know everybody in the world, but they're all His sons, so how can I judge? He can, because they are all His sons. *'So we let Your love decide what he, who You created as your son must be'*. So we let Him judge who we must be. And who are we? We're His son. The Son of God. The Source Himself. And there you have it.

# Truth Connection Fifty-Seven: ACIM Lesson 265 Explained.

Today I want to look at lesson 265 - 'Creation's gentleness is all I see'.

It goes on to say, 'I have indeed misunderstood the world, because I laid my sins on it and saw them looking back at me.'

This is about projection and reflection. What is projected out of your subconscious is reflected back at you. That is all it is saying. 'How fierce they seem', [the sins]. How fierce, how frightening, how scary, they seem... When really, they're not frightening at all. 'How deceived was I, to think that what I feared was in the world instead of in my mind alone'. What you fear in the world is actually only your mind projected out. You look around and see it reflected back at you. Your perception of what this world is, is what your mind judges it to be. The Lesson goes on to say, 'Today I see the world in celestial gentleness with which creation shines. There is no fear in it'. Which means you aren't projecting anything onto it. See it as it is. Try not to put your thoughts onto it.

All your thoughts are of the past and there is no past. What you think now are thoughts gained from your past and then used to make a future; a future based on fear. There is no past, so there is no fear, really – it is only what you want to put in it. *'Let no appearance of my sins obscure the light of Heaven shining on the world.'* My sins, or anybody's sins, are believing that this world is real. Once you know it is not real, you become sinless. What is reflected there is in God's mind. The images I see reflect my thoughts. You see, this is all made out of God, or the Source. Just like when you are dreaming at night, the people in your dream's environment are all you, aren't they? *'Yet is my mind at One with God's'.* What is reflected there is in God's mind - the images I see reflect my thoughts. Really, my mind is God's, therefore I can perceive creation's gentleness once I start to look for it. Lastly, is the prayer itself. *'In quiet would I look upon the world which but reflects your thoughts and mine as well. Let me remember that they are the same and I will see creation's gentleness.*

Remember that we are One with God. Don't look for your own thoughts. Look for God's thoughts, because you are One with them anyway, and really they are your thoughts. Don't think at all. Just look out on the world and enjoy.

# Truth Connection Fifty-Eight: Thoughts on ACIM Lesson 247.

Today's connection concerns lesson 247 - *'Without forgiveness I will still be blind'* It goes on to say, *'Sin is the symbol of attack. Behold it anywhere and I will suffer. For forgiveness is the only means whereby Christ's vision comes to me'*. When He says sin is the symbol of attack, He means sin as in believing all this to be real. That's all sin is. Believing this world to be real.

And when you believe it is real, it appears to attack you. So sin is the symbol of attack. *'Behold it anywhere and I will suffer'*. Because you look around thinking this is real, the guilt you suffer from past memories makes you think you're going to be punished, and it's going to come from some unknown direction, from who and from where, you do not know. But it's only because you are believing in the past that makes you think like that anyway. Sin is the symbol of attack, and it can be beheld potentially anywhere and everywhere, because the guilt in your subconscious makes you unwittingly fear any forthcoming punishment.

*'Now forgiveness is the only means whereby Christ's vision comes to me'*. Well, if you forgive all that stuff - by forgiving it, I mean

stop believing this is real - and stop thinking about the past or worrying about the future, you've only got right now and right now is fine. So just stay here and everything's cool.

*'Let me accept that His sight shows me the simple Truth and I'm healed completely. Then I don't see attack any more. Brother, (yourself), come and let me look on you. Your loveliness reflects my own. Your sinlessness is mine. You stand forgiven and I stand with you.'* This means that when you look on your brother, or anybody around you without the past to draw any references to, you see them as they really are. That's when you are at peace with them and yourself.

*'You stand forgiven and I stand with you.'* It goes on to say a short prayer, *'So I would look on everyone today, my brothers are your sons. Your fatherhood created them, as He created me, and you gave them all to me as part of you. My own self as well. Today, I honor you through them and thus I hope this day to recognize myself'*.

If I can see your innocence, the guiltlessness in you, then I must recognize it in myself. As you are my mirror and I see but myself in you.

# Truth Connection Fifty-Nine: What is Forgiveness?

What I want to talk about today is not strictly an ACIM lesson as such, but part of the introduction to Part Two, in between Lessons 220 and 221. It's the second part of the introduction and it is, 'What is forgiveness.' It is only one page long and it goes like this: *'Forgiveness recognizes what you thought your brother did to you has not occurred.'*

Which means true forgiveness - which is realizing this is all an illusion - and whatever I think my brother did to me never really happened, because the past doesn't exist. It's all a dream. Once it's moved off into the dreamed past, it hasn't happened.

It's only our memories that make you think anything has happened at all. So, forgiveness recognizes that what you thought your brother did to you has not occurred.

Forgiveness in the conventional earthly sense, does not pardon sins and actually makes them real. If I say to somebody who I think has wronged me, "Alright brother, I forgive you for stealing my money," in that sense, I'm actually acknowledging the 'sin' took place. If he thinks the 'sin' is real, by forgiving it that way, I'm admitting it is real too. I'm giving his perceived offence reality by forgiving him in the earthly way. Whereas, if I forgive him in the true way, I'm just recognizing that whatever he did was an illusion and he is totally forgiven and nobody's hurt at all. True forgiveness sees that there was no sin; because sin is only believing this is real.

Once you realize it is not real, you become sinless and in that view are all your sins forgiven. *'What is sin, but a false idea about God's son?'* Yes, an illusionary idea. That's the sin. True forgiveness merely sees its falsity and therefore lets it go. What then is free to take its place is the will of God. Once I've forgiven you by realizing it is an illusion, then the will of God can step in.

An unforgiving thought, where I am not going to forgive somebody for some perceived offence, is one that makes a judgment that I will refuse to doubt whether or not it is possibly untrue. People will say, "You did do that". Despite their protests concerning the perceived offence, you can insist that you are offended and no, no, no, you are not going to listen to reason and you are going to remain offended. Even though it is an illusion and it is not real—not true—you are still going to be offended. Therefore you are interacting with the illusion. The mind is closed and it will not be released. The thought protects projection. Tightening it's chains, so that distortions are more veiled, more obscured, less easily accessible to doubt and further kept from reason. It means that the unforgiving thought is keeping you in chains. You will not forgive that person. You will not realize that what he did is just a dream. So your interaction with the dream is causing you pain and suffering. What can come between a fixed projection and the aim that is chosen as its wanted goal? You are guilty and I want you punished. The only thing that can come between that fixed projection is True forgiveness.

*'An unforgiving thought does many things. In frantic action, it pursues its goal. Twisting and overturning what it sees as interfering with*

*its chosen path.'* It does not want to hear that is just an illusion. It wants the guilty party punished. *'Distortion is its purpose and the means by which it would accomplish it as well. It sets about its furious attempt to smash reality. Saying it isn't an illusion. It's true. Without concern for anything that would appear to pose a contradiction to its point of view.'*

It doesn't want to know that it is an illusion. It just wants punishment. *'Forgiveness, on the other hand, true forgiveness, is still and quietly does nothing. It offends no aspect of reality. Nor does it seek to twist it to the appearance it likes. It merely looks and waits and judges not.'*

Forgiveness. True forgiveness judges not. Because true forgiveness realizes that it is just an illusion. Oneness is True Reality.

*'He who would not forgive must judge. For he must justify his failure to forgive. But he who would forgive himself must learn to welcome Truth exactly as it is'.* You see, if you want to truly forgive, by recognizing this is an illusion, you have got to learn firstly that this *is* an illusion. You are born into a world where everybody believes this to be real. You're taught that this is 'real' and you have to undo that teaching. This undoing is called atonement. You have to achieve this atonement before you can see Reality. In Reality, this is just an illusion. *'Do nothing then. And let forgiveness show you what to do. Through Him who is your guide, your savior and protector. Strong in hope and certain of your ultimate success'.* The Holy Spirit in other words. Leave it up to Him. Because once you realize that this isn't real, there is no past. There's no future to worry about either.

You're in the now again. And in that time, you don't think. Just allow the Holy Spirit to come into you and let Him show you that this isn't Real. That it's just a dream to be enjoyed perfectly.

*'He has forgiven you already, for such is His function given Him by God. Now must you share His function, and forgive whom He has*

*saved. Who's sinlessness He sees and who He honors as the son of God'*. Meaning, you join with the Holy Spirit once you've stopped earthly forgiveness which is just interaction with the illusion. Once you've stopped doing that, you then become one with the Holy Spirit and see things as He does. In perfect peace and love. And that, is what True forgiveness is.

# Truth Connection Sixty: The End of the Dream.

Today I want to talk about lesson 226, *'My Home awaits me, I will hasten there'*.

It goes on to say, *'If I so choose, I can depart this world entirely. It is not death that makes this possible, but it is a change of mind about the purpose of the world'*. When He says 'change of mind,' He means awaken and realize this is an illusion. It is not death that makes departure possible. You depart from it by realizing you are in a dream. You're still here. Our passing (death) will take us beyond here, but the idea is to awaken while we're still here so we can appreciate the benefits of this wonderful place knowing that it is a dream. If you're dreaming at night and you suddenly realize that you're dreaming, all the fear disappears and you start having fun in the dream. Well, it's the same with this dream.

You must realize there's nothing to fear because it's all but a dream and all your dreams are born out of your memory. That's why it's so important to forget them. Because all they do is cause you trouble. And don't worry about the future. That's just pure worry.

It goes on to say, *'If I believe it has the value as I see it now, so will it still remain for me.'* The illusion will always be the same while you think it is an illusion. It is not until you waken and realize it is a dream that anything is going to change. There will always be negative things happening, then a positive thing happening, then a negative thing happening, then a positive thing happening. It just sways from side to side because it is a world of opposites. The negative is just as strong as the positive here. Whereas in Reality, there is only Perfect Love. There's no positive or negative.

The Lesson goes on to say, *'But if I see no value in the world as I behold it, nothing I want to keep as mine or search for as a goal, it will depart from me'*. It means this world as you see it will depart from you and you see it in a totally different way. This is because I have not sought for illusions to replace the Truth. The Truth has always been here. We've just been asleep. Well, we are still asleep. At least, the majority of the world is still asleep. The day is coming when everybody will awaken and that's the end of the dream. And then we're all home.

A small prayer follows: *'Father, my home awaits my glad return. Your arms are open and I hear your voice. What need have I to linger in a place of vain desires and shattered dreams when Heaven can so easily be mine?'* As I just said, awaken and Heaven is yours.

# Truth Connection Sixty-One: Love Loves to Love Love.

THE Lesson today is, *'All things I think I see reflect ideas.'* It goes on to say, *'This is salvation's keynote. What I see reflects a process in my mind which starts with my idea of what I want. From there the mind makes up an image of the thing the mind desires, judges it valuable and therefore seeks to find. These images are then projected outwards, looked upon, esteemed as real, and guarded as one's own.'*

This is the whole idea of projection and reflection and pretty much speaks for itself. When it says 'my own idea,' it doesn't mean, "I think I want this to happen, so it'll happen." You see, what reflects outwards comes from your subconscious. If you don't like somebody, it will reflect out of you and you will think people don't like you. Or certain people don't like you. If you don't like anybody, you will think everybody doesn't like you. If you love everybody, then you think everybody loves you. It's really quite simple. It is projection and reflection.

Your subconscious mind looks for the image it is projecting out. You might not know why you don't like somebody. A lot of people don't like the look of other people, when they don't even know the person. How can you not like somebody when you don't even know them? The subconscious decides not to like them, based on past memories. Maybe you have memories of someone who looks like this person, perhaps someone from the past who treated you badly. It's unfair on that person that you don't like them. They don't even know you don't like them, but your subconscious is projecting out onto them. It's seeking it out, and finding it, unfortunately.

It goes on to say, *'From insane wishes comes an insane world.'* These wishes are the wishes of the subconscious; an insane world where you are not liking people because of some projected subconscious thought. It's a judgment, actually.

*'From judgment comes a world condemned.'* You are judging this person, even though you don't know them. Based on past evidence that is just a memory of something that has nothing to do with them. *'From forgiving thoughts, loving thoughts, a gentle world comes forward. With mercy for the Holy Son of God'.* The son of God being your brother. *'To offer him a kindly home where he can rest a while before he journeys on and help his brothers walk ahead with him and find the way to Heaven to God.'* This means that if you forgive him, i.e. love him, you see him for what he truly is. Forget about what your memory is. Forget the past. See him for what he is. Your brother. Then you can help him to find God and he will then help you to find God. Without a past memory painted all over him, you can see him for what he really is, a True reflection of you. That's how we help each other find God and Heaven.

The short prayer at the bottom says, *'Our Father, your ideas reflect the Truth, and mine apart from yours, but make up dreams.'* It means, Father, our Source, has no past or future to worry about. He is just perfect Love. And if you can reflect that, which is Truth, then you are there. As it says here, *'...mine apart from yours, but make up dreams'*. My subconscious is making up dreams that I don't like these people based on past memories. It goes on to say, *'Let me behold what only yours reflect, for yours and yours alone, establish Truth'*. Well, that speaks for itself doesn't it? Yes it does.

# Truth Connection Sixty-Two:
# Black, White and Blue Men.

Living within our illusion of separation, one of the biggest problems we've got is everybody being separated into different races and colors. Now these different races and colors are all actually the same person, or the same being - the Source. We're simply within the mind of the Source having a dream.

For one person of a different color, saying to another person of a different color, they are different from him in some way, or somehow inferior to him in some way, that's plain ridiculous. It's like saying that one thing was better than another thing in the dream you had last night. How can it possibly be? It was all just a dream regardless of how anything appeared in the dream, it was still all just a dream.

Just as this is all just a dream. Separation is just a dream. Separated into black, white, yellow, red or whatever color people.

In a way, we're all blue men. Sad men; if we believe in separation. It's before our eyes, yes, but the only real thing is love. Nobody is separated. It doesn't matter what color they are. Looking down on somebody is wrong. Separation is wrong. It's true that we're separated into positive and negative, but that doesn't mean to say that we should look on people as being different. If you look at it positively, or look at it negatively, you'll find that positively is far, far closest to Godliness. Or the Source.

There's no such thing as separation. It's all a dream. And the idea of somebody believing they are better than another person is enforcing that dream. Enforcing that illusion. Nobody is better than anybody else. We're in a dream of separation and nothing more.

Underneath it all, we're just made out of Love. Perfect Love.

# Truth Connection Sixty-Three: ACIM Lesson 326. (I am Forever an Effect of God) Ideas Cannot Leave Their Source.

The lesson begins, 'Father, I was created in your mind, a Holy thought that never left its home. I am forever your effect and you forever and ever, are my cause.'

This is about cause and effect. Ideas never leave their source. If I have an idea, I can share it with somebody, but it's always my idea. It can never leave me. It is the same with the Source. We are His idea. So it cannot leave Him. We cannot leave Him. We only think we can. We are dreaming. '*As you created me, I have remained.*' As I've just said, we are His idea, but we're dreaming we are not.

'*Wherever you establish me, I still abide. I am established in the mind of the Source.*' I am actually still there, although I am dreaming that I am not. '*… and all your attributes abide in me, because it is your will to have a son so like his cause that cause and effect are indistinguishable*'.

I mean, really, if I have an idea, the idea is me, isn't it? If I share it with somebody it is still my idea. The idea is me. Just as I, as the Source's idea, am Him.

*'Let me know that I am an effect of God, and so I have the power to create like you'.* I create what is around me. Like Him, what I project reflects back at me and I have created it. *'And as it is in Heaven, so on earth. Your plan I follow here and at the end I know that you will gather your effects into the tranquil Heaven of your love. Where earth will vanish and all separate thoughts unite in glory as the son of God'.* As He says, 'and as it is in Heaven, so on earth', around me are my creations, just as in Heaven are the Source's creations.

*'Your plan I follow here and at the end I know that you will gather your effects into the tranquil Heaven of your love.'* Once I recognize I am dreaming, then the Source can gather me back to my rightful place in Heaven. Or gather us all back, as we are all His sons and once we all recognize that, we're all Home. Into the tranquil Heaven of His love. Where earth will vanish. That means, once I realize I am dreaming - or once everybody realizes they are dreaming - that is the end of the dream. The end of earth.

*'And all the separate thoughts that we have, will unite as the Son of God.'* They will reunite as One. The son of God. The Son of the Source. Us and our Cause. Us, the effect, will reunite with God, or the Source, our Cause. *'So let us today, behold earth disappear, at first transformed, and then, forgiven, fade entirely into God's - or the Source's - Holy will.'* We must recognize that we are not of the earth. At first we are transformed when we realize we are actually God, or the Source, ourselves and then forgiven. Forgiven as in recognizing this is a dream, and then fade entirely into God's holy will. We become one with God again. One with the Source again. We are reunited with Truth and back in our Home. We are still here on earth, so to speak, but now, we know the Truth. That lesson is all about recognizing that we are an idea in the mind of God and that ideas never leave their source.

# Truth Connection Sixty-Four: At the Borderland - Awakening to Truth.

Today I'd like to talk about some very nice quotes from A Course in Miracles. They are from Chapter 26, *'The Transition,'* Part 3, *'The Borderland.'* It begins by saying complexity is not of God. How could it be when all He knows is One? It really speaks for itself, doesn't it? How can Oneness be complex? In this opposing world we live in, everything is endlessly complex, but eventually the dream itself will end.

It being a dream about separation, everything in it keeps separating and separating and separating into the complex chaos we live in now. He (God) knows of One creation, One reality, One Truth and but One Son.

Nothing conflicts with Oneness. That's His One creation. This existence is all one in Truth. It is only in our dream that we are seeing everything as separate. On awakening, it still looks the same, but we know it isn't separate. It's really One. One Reality. One Truth. One Son. They are all the same thing. The son being us, the fragmented son of God. There's millions of us walking the earth. Perhaps even on other planets, but actually we're all one being in the mind of God, or the Source.

The Truth is simple. It is One without an opposite. It goes on to say there is a borderland of thought that stands between this world and Heaven. It is not a place and when you reach it, it is apart from time. Here is the meeting place where thoughts are brought together, where conflicting values meet and all illusions are laid down beside the Truth where they are judged to be untrue.

It means you wake up and it's all been a dream. All these thoughts you've ever had, the guilty and painful thoughts of the past and worried thoughts about the future, were all just nothing. We're in a dream that was never anything. Anybody's thoughts were never anything or of any importance. We thought they were, because we thought this is real, but it's not. Once you realize it's not real, your thoughts become unimportant. Sin is believing this is 'real'. The sinless are those who know it isn't. That borderland He speaks of is the awakening. You haven't passed on, but you've woken up and you are still here. That's why it says this borderland is just beyond the gate of Heaven. You're nearly Home. You're nearly at Oneness.

# Truth Connection Sixty-Five: The Dreamer and the Dreamed.

I would like to elaborate a little further about us being in an illusion. Just like, or akin to, the people in our night time dreams.

The people in our night time dreams do just as they like. They have the free will to do just as they want, the same as we do here in the illusion. We have free will and we do as we please within the mind of the Source.

To gain an understanding of this, let us consider what would happen if someone in your night time dreams turned to you and said, "Hey. What is it like to be 'real'?" What would you say?

You could say, "Well, it is like you, except 'real'." They'd ask, "What is 'real'?" You'd have to say, "In your current state, you can't understand what it's like to be 'real' because you are just a person my dreams. You are separated from me. You're looking at me from within the confines of the dream. Are you seeing me? I don't know, but you're speaking to me as if I exist. So you must realize that I exist, and I am making you. I have something to do with your existence and I am dreaming you." Perhaps they would respond, "I don't believe that. That would mean I am you." You would say, "Don't you feel like you are me?" and they would say, "Not really, I feel disconnected from you. I feel separated." You could say, "That's only because you are part of my dream. You're not separated. You are me, really."

They may then say, "I am you - how can I be you?" But you know that they are you and any doubts they may have are of no consequence.

Will that person in the dream ever figure out that they are actually me? It doesn't matter, but far better, I'd say, to tell them they'll find out soon enough on my/their waking and that there is no need to be fearful within the dream they're in, for not only is it not 'real', but they have their True identity in me to look forward to, and beyond that, *my* True identity. It all gets better and better.

You could tell them that for sure.

# Truth Connection Sixty-Six: Illusions, Truth and the Wholly (Holy) Spirit.

This connection concerns the nature of Truth and I would like to discuss it using quotes from Lesson 107 from A Course in Miracles. *'Truth will correct all errors in my mind.'*

It goes on to say, *'What can correct illusions but the Truth?'* Illusions are just untruths. Illusion is not real.

It continues, *'They are gone because without belief they have no life.'* When you are dreaming at night, while you're believing the dream to be 'real', you just go along with it, you don't question what you see. Whereas here, you do question what you see. You make judgments all the time.

The lesson then says, *'They're gone because without belief they have no life'*. Once you awaken and realize you were just dreaming, it has no life. It just becomes the emptiness it always was. Without illusions there could be no fear, no doubt and no attack. In Truth, there *is* no fear, no doubt and no attack. The Truth is Oneness. That we are all One. Anything outside that is untruth.

Separation. We are not separated. Separation itself is untruth and anything to do with it is untruth.

'When Truth is come, all pain is over. For there is no room for transitory thoughts and dead ideas to linger in your mind'. When truth is come all pain is over, because all those guilty things you thought you did, Truth will come and show you that they were never so and all is well.

The dead ideas. They were never real. The Truth will stop that. Transitory thoughts. Changing your mind. There is nothing to change your mind about. The truth is just Oneness. It doesn't change to anything. Which takes me to this next quote, *'When Truth has come, it does not stay a while, disappear, or change to something else'.*

In this world of change and separation, all that is around us is constantly changing. Not one second of existence within this world is the same as it was the second before. A bird has flown a little bit further on. A fish has dived a little deeper into the sea. A car moves closer to the motorway's exit. Your breath is further from your mouth but a second later. Everything is in constant movement. So how can it be true? The Truth stays constant. Eternally, it is always the truth. How can something that keeps changing to something else be True? At what moment is it ever True? Think on.

When Truth has come, it does not stay a while, disappear, or change to something else. *'It does not shift and alter in its form, or come and go and then come again. It stays exactly as it always was. To be depended on in every need and trusted with a perfect trust in all the seeming difficulties and all that the doubts and appearances in the world engender. They will merely blow away when Truth corrects the errors in your mind. Everything you ever thought. Everything that ever frightened you, will just be blown away with the Truth'.* They never were. It goes on to say later, *'We do not ask for what we do not have. We merely ask for what belongs to us that we may recognize it as our own. And what belongs to us is the perfect peace that comes with Truth'.* It is ours and it is within us now. It's just that we've put up this wall between us and this perfect peace. This illusion, which disturbs us endlessly, will end when we finally recognize it is a dream. This lesson is actually for a person to remember every day to say *'Truth will correct all errors in my mind and I will rest in Him who is myself. Do not forget your function for today. Each time you tell yourself with confidence, "Truth will correct all errors in my mind," you speak for all the world and Him who would release the world as he would set you free'.*

The 'He' referred to is the Holy Spirit. This is the part of the mind of the Source that understands your predicament and He is the one who mediates between the Source and us.

The Source, being Oneness, doesn't understand this separation. It's not His idea. We are the dreamers. Although we are part of Him, we are the ones experiencing the dream. Once we awaken, we re-join Him. But until then, we have to ask the Holy Spirit (or whatever name you want to call Him). That conduit, between us and the Source, is the One that is taking us Home. If we allow ourselves to see through His eyes, we will see nothing but the perfect Truth of Oneness, and that nobody's separated.

We're all connected by Love and He can take charge and take us Home.

# Truth Connection Sixty-Seven: There is No Death.

This connection is in response to a request from a brother to say a few words about dying.

Nobody dies.

Dying is something that happens in the illusion, because everything here, being opposites, has a beginning and it has to have an end. Or the end of the function of the body as the end of us.

It is not the end at all. It is just the end of the dream. In fact, it is not a dying, it is an awakening. A beginning of being Home again. It was only ever a temporary thing. Remember, at Home it is Eternity. This is just a visit. If you know you're going to leave here soon, it's just the end of the trip, that's all. The body itself is actually like a kind of receiver. Everybody receives the signals and sees them differently. Do you remember the old days when you used to get rows of television sets in shop windows and you'd look at all these TV sets and there would be significant variations on the screens? They'd all have the same program on, but some would be more brightly colored than others. One might be in black and white, one might have more green in it, one might be more sharp, another one might be more clearly focused than the one next to it. Looking at these TV sets, you could see distinct differences in all of them, even though they are all showing the same program.

Well, it's pretty much the same with us. We're all showing, or seeing, the same program, but we're all translating it as it is for us within the workings of our brain, just as it is within the workings of the TV set that presents the received image on the screen. We're just the same as that. We're tuned into a certain frequency to see this world. Presumably there must be millions, zillions, countless other frequencies like there are channels on a TV set. But really, it is all an illusion. Every single bit of it. Once a TV set packs up and doesn't work anymore, it doesn't matter to the TV signal. That's there regardless of the TV set. It doesn't know if the TV set is working, finished, alive, not working or whatever.

What is important is the signal in the air. Not the set itself. All the set does is receive and transmit and we are the same. We're just that signal. That invisible signal. The Truth is what we really are. The Truth is that we are all One. One Spirit. The mind of God. Like the characters in our night time dreams being us, we, in the mind of God, are Him. There is no dying. It is but an awakening to Truth

# TRUTH CONNECTION SIXTY-EIGHT: ALL ARE ONE AND ALL ARE WORTHY.

SOMEONE once said to me, that on realizing they must be a character in a dream, they then realized they must be the character whose dream they are inside of, so to speak. If I dream about somebody, they are actually me. Even though they appear to be separate inside my head, they're not. They're me.

That's the same as us within the mind of the Source; in His idea, or dream, or illusion, whatever you like to call it, we are characters in His mind, just like the characters in our night time dreams. Upon realizing that that is the case, that we are God or the Source ourselves, there are some who suddenly feel very unworthy, like it couldn't be true. How can we be God? Or the Source? Or any such Entity? Or this great energy that we all are - how could that be? If you are within the mind of the Source, being dreamed about by the Source, you must be the Source. If it walks like a duck, talks like a duck...

It takes a while for that realization to sink in for some. But it's true. Why do people feel unworthy? Because there's so much negativity in this world to put it to them that they are - and they are bombarded with it - so they end up believing it. This is the world of the great deceiver. And what a great deceiver he is, the ego. If you are believing you are not worthy, you've been deceived. But the great news is, you can become undeceived. Endeavor to stop thinking about your past. Never think about the future. Just stay in the now. Before very long, your very own great worth will dawn on you and you'll realize just who you really are. Truly.

# Truth Connection Sixty-Nine:
# The Dreamer and the Dream are One.

Today I want to talk about a single line in ACIM's Chapter 28, *'The Undoing of Fear'*, in part IV, *'The Greater Joining'*. It is part four of the fifth paragraph and it says, *'Identity in dreams is meaningless, because the dreamer and the dream are One'*.

In my night time dreams everybody and everything in it are one with me. When I'm dreaming I think it is real, and I make a kind of sense out of it because I inherently know what things are. You know that's a tree in your dream or a table in your dream or some other person you may or not know walking past in a dream. Someone you know in so-called reality walks past and you think of them as a name. But when you wake up, it's you. Or me, rather, in my dream. It was just me.

The dreamer and the dream are one.

What He is saying there, is the same as this dream within the mind of the Source. Everything in it is one with the Source because the Source is just Oneness. Here, in the dream, we're dreaming we're separate and labeling and naming everything and thinking that it is real, when it's not. It's a dream. On waking from the dream, we will realize we've been only dreaming we were separated all this time, and although it all still looks the same, we now know that we are one with the Source, or God. And when you know that, you awaken and there's nothing more to fear because fear is born of what we imagine to be going on in this dream.

The newspapers, television and radio - how often do they have anything positive to talk about? For them, it's all about the negative aspects of the dream and because the dream is the opposite of the positivity of God, it contains one hell of a lot of negativity. But really, it isn't anything. It's just a dream. Just like my dreams last night. The dreamer and the dream are one. And we ALL are One.

# Truth Connection Seventy: A Tale of Labels and Tables.

Today I want to revisit the subject of naming all that which is around us; our unwittingly hanging labels on things so that we identify with this world and create some kind of understanding of what it actually is. What it really is, as I've said in earlier connections, is just an illusionary stage complete with scenery and props. Any meaning it has is what we ourselves attach to it. That goes for the value of it as well. A piece of gold, when all is said and done, is just a piece of rock. Those who are concerned about such things have to keep it scarce as the more scarce it is, the more valuable this rock is. It's all a bit odd, really.

Everything here has value as we accord it. Take this story for example: A fellow goes into an antique shop and he sees an antique table. This table costs a thousand dollars, but he doesn't care, he recognizes it as a Louis XIV French table and he wants it for his collection. He wants it in his salon.

So he gives the dealer a thousand dollars and he takes it home and gives it pride of place in his living room. Pure Louis the XIV (valuable).

Anyway, one day he invites some friends round and one them says, "Where did you get that table?"

He replies, "I bought it in an antique shop, cost me a thousand dollars." His friend says, "I'm afraid you've been done, mate. This is a fake."

"What?!"

"This is a fake. I've come across lots of them. They're turned out in a factory somewhere and are worth about twenty dollars at the most - you've been really done mate, sorry."

"Oh."

Anyway, they all eventually go home and he's left there, staring at his now worthless table, thinking, "Oh no. How could I be so foolish?" Far from gazing at it with love and wonder, as before, he now looks at it as some worthless object. Such is his disappointment he takes the table and goes and puts it in a spare room and forgets about it.

About a month later, some other friends come round and he starts telling them about how he was 'done' buying this table and one of his friends asks if he can have a look at it.

He shows him the table, and his friend says, "Look, your friend doesn't know what he's talking about. This is a genuine Louis the XIV piece of furniture. I've studied this kind of stuff all my life and I'm telling you this is the real thing. Disregard what he says. He doesn't know what he is talking about."

All of a sudden, the guy looks at his table once more anew, and once again he sees it in awe and wonder. He marvels at it's very Louis XIV-ness, as he did once before, it's worth reinstated.

But really, the table itself has not a clue about the worth that has been accorded to it. Or even what has been going on. The table, being made of wood, is actually only a table because we've put some pieces of timber together and called it a table. Really it's just some pieces of wood. In essence, solely wood. We cut it into pieces and hang labels on all the components and fit it all together and it becomes a table. And a table only because you've hung labels on all the bits.

It's still just wood, and you see, as with everything here, the only value it has is what we choose to place on it.

# Truth Connection Seventy-One: God does not forgive? Of course He does. ACIM Lesson 46 Explained.

The first couple of paragraphs explain what it's about and I just want to run through that first. *'God is the love in which I forgive,'* is the title.

Firstly, it says, *'God does not forgive, because He has never condemned'*. This means that God does not need to forgive. He knows that this isn't real, so what has he got to forgive? It's us who have got to forgive. He has never condemned. (In this context, 'condemned' means thinking that this is real.)

*'And there must be condemnation before forgiveness is necessary'*.

Cause and effect again. Something has to be taken as wrong before it can be forgiven.

*'Forgiveness is the great need of this world. But that is because it is a world of illusions'*.

If it is an illusion, it is not right and it needs forgiving by realizing that it is wrong. It is an illusion.

*'Those who forgive are thus releasing themselves from illusions'.*

Because they realize they are in a dream, *'while those who withhold forgiveness are binding themselves to them'.*

Most people who insist that this is real only think that because their conditioning tells them so. At present, they just can't get their heads around something like this. That's what the whole of A Course in Miracles is about; it educates teachers to be able to go out to the masses.

Further, it says *'As you condemn only yourself, so do you forgive only yourself'.*

You are condemning yourself by believing this to be real. Only you can forgive yourself, by recognizing it is not.

*'Yet, although God does not forgive, His love is nevertheless the basis of forgiveness'.*

Even though he doesn't know about forgiveness, His love is nevertheless the basis of forgiveness, because it is loving someone enough to overlook any animosity you may have, to see beyond it and realize that it is just a dream and he is just a figure in a dream. He's only really hurt you because you believed he had.

*'Fear condemns and love forgives'.*

If you are fearful, you are interacting with the dream. For example: you can hold your head in despair upon hearing the terrible news stories on the television or radio. You let the stories affect you.

But it is purely interaction with the illusion. I'm not saying you should ignore the plight of what is going on in the world's affairs, but you should look upon it all as an observer; a concerned observer, rather than taking it to heart and having negative thoughts yourself. If you interact, the dream is winning.

There's positive and negative in this dream. The negative bit is a real nightmare. You've probably noticed.

*'Forgiveness thus undoes what fear has produced, returning the mind to the awareness of God'.*

Once you realize that here, like the illusion, isn't real, you return to the awareness of God, who knows that nothing here is real. For this reason, forgiveness can truly be called salvation. It is the means by which illusions disappear.

# Truth Connection Seventy-Two: Forgiving and Forgetting - Refreshing the Mind.

In this connection, I want to talk about one of my favorite passages in ACIM and that is from the Text, Chapter 31, *'The Final Vision'*. It's the last passages from the first part, *'The Simplicity of Salvation'*, parts 12 and 13. It is so very profound, I think.

*'Let us be still an instant and forget all things we ever learned'* - which is the past, isn't it?

*'All thoughts we had and every preconception that we hold of what things mean and what their purpose is. Let us not remember our own ideas of what the world is for. We do not know'*.

We've only got our own ideas of what the world is for. We don't know what it is for. We just make our own world up, hang all the labels on it, name everything, add some drama and there's our life. But really, we don't know what it is.

*'Let every image held of everyone be loosened from our minds and swept away'*.

This refers to any preconceived ideas we had of what people were like. How can you possibly know somebody by what they show to you? Only you truly know yourself, ego-wise, and that goes for everybody else.

*'Be innocent of judgment, unaware of any thoughts of evil or of good that ever crossed your mind about anyone'* - Just forget everything - *'Now do you know him not'*.

No, you don't know your brother. It means that you've thrown away all preconceived ideas about him and now you see your brother anew.

*'But you are free to learn of him, and learn of him anew. Now is he born again to you, and you are born again to him, without the past that sentenced him to die, and you with him'.*

Where it says, '….sentenced him to die,' it doesn't mean this literally; it means with what you've laid on him, your ideas about what he was. They aren't true. It's just your ideas of what he is, so you've sentenced him to die, in the sense of what you're saying of him is not the truth. You've sentenced him to be within the illusion. Where he will eventually 'die'.

*'Now he is free to live as you are free, because an ancient learning passed away and left a place for the truth to be reborn'.*

My old thoughts about him and about everything else must be done away with. While I am harboring all these memories and preconceived ideas about what the person may or may not be, which aren't true anyway, they are blocking off the real truth from entering my consciousness about what my brother really is.

It's all in the mind.

# Truth Connection Seventy-Three: Understanding the True Nature of Cause and Effect.

From ACIM Chapter 27, *'The Healing of the Dream'*, part III *'Beyond all Symbols'*.

*'The picture of the brother you see, means nothing. There is nothing to attack or deny, to love or hate or to endow with power or to see as weak'.*

It's saying basically that the picture of my brother - the person standing before me - is an illusion. What I perceive of him is my own personal idea, based on my memories of what he is or what he is like. It is only my perception of what he is, so it is not true. It means nothing.

*'There is nothing to attack or deny, to love or hate or to endow with power or to see as weak'.*

I start 'adding' to the person I see before me. I know nothing about him, the truth of him, so everything that I see about him are things that I've added to him. Maybe I will decide that he is weak or untrustworthy or strong and of a happy disposition. I might decide to love him or maybe I will hate him.

It is all my decision. He is just there in his illusionary way.

It says then, '*The picture has been wholly cancelled out because it symbolized a contradiction that cancelled out the thought it represents*'. It is talking about cause and effect. You see, in our world, which opposes Truth, we think the unreal is True.

The unreal being this: *We see the world around us as the cause and ourselves as the effect. All of the problems we encounter come from this world around us. It's the cause and what it does to us is the effect.*

Well, that's not the Truth. The Truth is the other way round - we are the cause and this is the effect. What we project out is the cause and what we see around us is the effect. How I see my brother is the cause I projected out, the effect is how I see him.

But it is only a thought that I project out onto the illusion itself, i.e. my brother standing before me. It's not what he really is.

It's something like the Rushmore Memorial in America, where they have those four US presidents carved out of a mountain. Lots of tourists go there and look at it, but really all they're looking at is just one great big rock. The fact that there's four presidents depicted on it is an illusion. They're really looking at images grown familiar through individual memories. Behind that chiseled facade is just rock and what they are actually looking at are the Black Hills of Dakota. Any idea of image is solely in their heads. In reality, that which stands before them is just an illusion caused by very skilled sculptors.

The chapter goes on to say, '*....and thus the picture has no cause at all*'. Once I see that I have caused my brother's image, that it has no cause at all, that it is just a thought of mine, I can then look beyond that for what he really is.

'*The picture of the brother you see is wholly absent and never has been*'.

It's never been there. What is there is what we have put there. What I have put there.

*'Let then the empty space it occupies be recognized as vacant and the time devoted to its seeing be perceived as idly spent, a time unoccupied. An empty space that is not seen as filled, an unused interval of time not seen as spent but fully occupied, becomes a silent invitation for the Truth to enter and to make itself at home'.*

Once I've stopped seeing my brother as the illusionary being I project onto him, then God can step in and show me what he really is - an extension of Himself; just as I am. Oneness. It is there for us all to see.

We simply have to work at it. The reward is beyond valuable.

# Truth Connection Seventy-Four: Waking to Redemption.

From ACIM Chapter 11 in the Text, *'God or the Ego'*. Part VI *'Waking to redemption'*.

It begins, *'It is impossible not to believe what you see'*.

You look around and see the world and it is impossible not to believe it. We take it to be real, because we know no different. It is impossible not to believe what you see.

*'But it is equally impossible to see what you do not believe'*.

What does that mean? If someone is talking to you and you know that they are lying, you can't believe what they are saying. Even though it is their view, you can't believe what you do not believe. You can't *see* his point of view. If he is spinning you a yarn, he's telling you a story that he wants you to believe, but you can't *see* it. You don't believe it, so you'll never *see* that story. You'll not see it as Truth, so you don't believe it. Therefore, by saying it is impossible not to believe what you see (which it isn't), it is equally impossible to see what you do not believe. Once you know that this world is a lie, you can't believe this either. By 'lie', I mean illusion.

Perceptions are built up on memories and experience, and these lead to beliefs.

If I make my mind up I don't like somebody, and every time I see them I don't like them, it's from an experience or memory where they offended me and I decided I don't like them, and I hold that view all the time.

I don't like them. But really, how can that be a true view? It is my decided view, my perceived view of what this man is like. His friends and family do not see him that way.

This is a fictitious person, by the way. I love everybody now.

*'It is not until beliefs are fixed that perceptions stabilize'*, and that is exactly what I am saying there.

In effect, what you believe, you do see. What I believe about someone that I decide I don't like, is that I see him as dislikeable. The Author goes on to say, *'That is what I meant when I said "blessed are ye who have not seen, yet still believe"'*.

Blessed are those who have yet to awaken to the Reality of Truth and yet still believe that it's there. They are seeing the lie, the illusion, yet they know the Truth is within it waiting to be found.

A person sees it whether they like it or not, but it is your choice how you see it. An awakened man sees it as it truly is.

It goes on to say, *'For those who believe in the resurrection will see it. The Truth'*.

The resurrection being the risen Christ. *'The resurrection is the complete triumph of Christ over the ego'*. Christ being 'knowledge' in that sense. Jesus Christ = Jesus with the knowledge. The complete triumph of knowledge over the ego. The knowledge of Truth. Christ is Truth, and that is the triumph of Truth over the ego - not by attack, but by transcendence; by rising above it.

*'But Christ does rise above the ego and all its works'*. This could read as the devil and all his works. *'And ascends to the father in his kingdom'*.

He ascends to the Truth.

# Truth Connection Seventy-Five: Miracles

Here I refer to chapter one, the very first chapter in the book, *A Course in Miracles*, 'The Meaning of Miracles', and it is the first part, 'The Principles of Miracles'. There are fifty principles, but here I want to discuss those of them that stand out in particular for me.

The first is the third one: *'Miracles occur naturally as expressions of love. The real miracle is the love that inspires them. In this sense, everything that comes from love is a miracle'.*

Love is God. God is Love. Love comes from God and miracles *are* God. So that's pretty self-explanatory, that one. Anything that comes from Love is a miracle. If you are kind enough to help somebody out who is poor, desperate or in trouble, for them it is a miracle.

The eighth principle: *'Miracles are healing because they supply a lack; they are performed by those who temporarily have more for those who temporarily have less'.* If a beggar in the street has nothing to eat and nothing to drink and then someone comes along, gives him some money and says "Here you are mate, get yourself a cup of tea and a cake." For him that's a miracle.

The tenth principle: *'The use of miracles as spectacles to induce belief is a misunderstanding of their purpose'*. That brings to mind the story of Christ walking in water. That must have been some spectacle. What would He want to do that for? Whether He did or not, I really don't know, but according to some accounts, he did just that in order to rescue one of His disciples, so it was an act of Love. Miracles *are* Love. It is not for the purpose of amusement of yourself or others.

The Sixteenth Principle: *'Miracles are teaching devices for demonstrating it is as blessed to give as it is as to receive. They simultaneously increase the strength of the giver and supply strength to the receiver'*. That is because within Oneness, that which God is, what Jesus is, what we all Truly are, giving and receiving are the same. Everything is One. I'm the same as you. I *am* you back home in Oneness. It might cost you a lot of money to help somebody who is struggling, but when you see the happiness and relief you have brought about for them, you get all that happiness and reflected, multiplied, back at you. Happiness is worth a lot more than money. Infinitely more.

The Twenty-Fourth Principle: *'Miracles enable you to heal the sick and raise the dead because you made sickness and death yourself, and can therefore abolish both. You are a miracle, capable of creating in the likeness of your Creator. Everything else is your own nightmare, and does not exist. Only the creations of light are real'*. When you know that this is a dream, you can do anything. Jesus knew our existence here is a dream absolutely, and He could do absolutely anything. Note however, that in the Bible, He did it for people who believed in Him. Like the Roman soldier who asked Him to come and help his poorly servant, and Jesus says that He will come with him. The Roman soldier replied that Jesus didn't need to. He would only have to say that the servant is healed and he would be healed. Jesus said that never had He seen such faith and that for the soldier to go home as his trust had made the servant well again. And he was. That's the sort of faith we are talking about here - the *miracles* we are talking about here. Anybody can perform them - once they've awoken, and awoken truly.

The Twenty-Sixth Principle: *'Miracles represent freedom from fear. "Atoning" means "undoing." The undoing of fear is an essential part of the atonement value of miracles'*. The undoing of fear - the getting rid of guilt.

The Thirty-Ninth Principle: *'The miracle dissolves error because the Holy Spirit identifies error as false or unreal. This is the same as saying that by perceiving light, darkness automatically disappears'*. The miracle dissolves error, because the miracle is Truth and the illusion is untruth. Once you see the light of God all the darkness around you disappears. Error, the illusion, disappears. Error is something that isn't as it should be. An illusion is something that isn't as it should be - and the miracle dissolves it. Brings Truth to it.

The Forty-Fifth Principle: *'A miracle is never lost. It may touch many people you have not even met, and produce undreamed of changes in situations of which you are not even aware'*. A miracle can be very small. You could be walking along the street and see somebody looking sad, and you may smile at them and they may smile back. That person may have had nothing to smile about all day long and then suddenly you've given them something to smile at. Your passing gesture may have cheered them just enough to change their mind about doing something drastic. Miracles can be that small. Yet there is no order of size in miracles. In a dream big miracles are the same as little miracles. Amazing things happen in dreams. Amazing things can happen here.

The Author speaks about waking the dead. I have to say that in my experience, I haven't yet come across anybody performing such an act. But then again, I'm not absolutely awakened like Jesus was. I am awakened enough however, to know that these words are Truth - and that is an excellent start.

# Truth Connection Seventy-Six: Bringing Truth to illusions.

I've mentioned it briefly in earlier connections, but here I would like to discuss a more advanced way of dealing with guilty thoughts from the past. I've previously discussed the plucking of these unwanted thoughts from your mind; stopping thinking about them altogether and getting rid of painful memories in general. They are good, useful ways of dealing with the problem, but there is available to you a more definite and advanced way.

Once you've learned to control your mind enough to cast out those thoughts, here is a way of dealing with them completely as there is a chance they can will stay hidden in the background of your mind and fester. I know you're not thinking about them, but they can stay rooted there in the background causing upset in a way you aren't realizing is happening. You might be quick to anger about something and not understand why it is so. In cases like this, it is generally down to these thoughts not being completely dissolved. Some people manage to do away with these bad thoughts altogether just by plucking them from their minds, but generally it is a good idea to bring the Truth to these old memories.

You know when an attacking thought has sneaked into your mind because you start to feel unhappy - feel guilty - feel anxious. What you can do is firstly bring the offending scenario completely to mind. I know it can be very painful to do this and that's why a lot of people don't like using this idea in the first instance. It can be quite agonising to start with and that's why I believe it is best to have a certain degree of mind mastery before you can attempt it. There is nothing stopping you trying though. You may find it easier than some.

What you do is bring Jesus with you to this memory. Imagine yourself within the offending memory and also imagine that Jesus, or the Holy Spirit is standing alongside you. He is the Truth. He is bringing the Truth to your illusion. Say to Him, "Jesus, this is a dream isn't it?" What do you think He is going to say? He will turn to you and say, "Of course it is. Forget it."

And you know what? That old memory will then just dissolve away, there and then. If there is such a case where the memory sneaks back into your head again, ask Jesus again. He won't mind. That's what He's here for. He'll return gladly, and He'll help you dissolve those bad, guilty and wholly unnecessary thoughts completely.

The plucking of bad thoughts from your mind is a more straightforward idea to administer, but as I've said, once you've gained a stronger control of your thoughts, ask Jesus, or the Holy Spirit (They are the same really) to come with you and He will help you. That way there is nothing left rotting in the depths of your mind causing you pains you are often unaware of until they are stirred. A 'new broom' sweeping clean. A clean mind will bring you atonement.

An undoing.

Awakening.

# Truth Connection Seventy-Seven:
# Above all Else I Want to See.

The whole idea of A Course in Miracles is to get everybody to see the Truth; to see through the illusion and see it for what it really is - the Oneness that it really is. We see this dream of separation and act like we are separated, because we don't know any better. The idea of the Course is to help you to see the Truth and lesson 27, *Above All Else I Want To See*, is centered exactly on that. This idea expresses something stronger than mere determination. It gives vision priority among your desires. The purpose of today's exercise is to bring the time when the idea will be wholly true a little nearer. The exercise is just to repeat as often as you can today, ideally every half-hour or even better, every 15 or 20 minutes, "Above all else I want to see."

Once you know that this is an illusion, the Source, or God, takes the last step. He opens your eyes for you. He will confirm to you that this is truly Oneness and not the dream of separation you always believed it was. Some people are afraid of such a notion. They think the world will look so different, it will scare them. He covers that by asking you to say to yourself, "*Vision has no cost to anyone,*" along with, "Above all else I want to see". Also, '*It can only bless*', is a useful addition.

We can be compared to the people who inhabit your night time dreams. When you wake up, what happens to them? It doesn't matter. They were you anyway and now you're awake. It is just the same here. We awaken to God and realize that we are Him. What can be bad about that?

It further says in the Lesson that the real question is how often will you remember to say 'Above all else I want to see?' How much do you want today's idea to be true? Answer one of these questions and you've answered the other. Obviously the more you remember to say it, the more you want it to be true.

The last sentence says, *'If only once during the day, you feel that you were perfectly sincere while you were repeating today's idea, you can be sure that you have saved yourself many years of effort.'* Every time you say it, it becomes more and more concrete in your mind. "Above all else I want to see." Just keep saying it. Keep thinking it to yourself. When you wake up in the morning and before you go to bed at night. Any time. Get something to hang around your neck, so that whenever you touch it, you remember to say it.

"Above all else I want to see". Keep saying it. Because one day, you will see. And then you're Home. You are Home without passing on and then you can enjoy this place as it was always meant to be enjoyed. As the Son of God.

## THE END

www.ingramcontent.com/pod-product-compliance
Lightning Source LLC
Chambersburg PA
CBHW050538300426
44113CB00012B/2157